DEVIL MAN ON ROUTE 66

A Memoir by Terry G.

NVus Media Productions

Devil Man On Route 66
A Memoir by Terry G.
All Rights Reserved.
Copyright © 2022 Terry G.
v2.0

The opinions expressed in this manuscript are solely the opinions of the author and do not represent the opinions or thoughts of the publisher. The author has represented and warranted full ownership and/or legal right to publish all the materials in this book.

This book may not be reproduced, transmitted, or stored in whole or in part by any means, including graphic, electronic, or mechanical without the express written consent of the publisher except in the case of brief quotations embodied in critical articles and reviews.

NVus Media Productions

ISBN: 978-0-578-26630-5

Library of Congress Control Number: 2022909049

Cover Photo © 2022 Terry G. All rights reserved - used with permission.

PRINTED IN THE UNITED STATES OF AMERICA

Acknowlegements

This book is dedicated to my family, both biological and adopted. My adopted family molded me into the man I am today. They gave me all the traits that I am most proud of. I can see how each one of them contributed to my personality.

My mother and father gave me values, taught me to respect others and to treat everyone around me like I want to be treated. My mother taught me that words and a piece of paper can be more artistic than a picture or song. My father taught me to do an honest, hard day's work and that to do so is like life's built-in therapy. It is something to be proud of and to do the absolute best possible each day without taking advantage of others. I am so glad he instilled that quality in me!

My three adopted sisters taught me to dream big, love life, and how to be responsible socially. They each contributed to my musical foundation, early in life, in many beautiful ways. I have tons of fond memories hearing the music that each sister played throughout my childhood. All the adopted family taught me to laugh and smile. They taught me to look forward to the next day, the next accomplishment, and that the power to be the best at whatever I aspired to do or learn was easily within my grasp. Thank you for your unconditional love and attention guys! You are the greatest!

I think another huge debt of gratitude belongs to Denise, my wife of over 30 years, my children Michelle, Alexander, Parker, Hayden, and Arlen. Also, to my grandchildren (4 currently). I am super proud of all of you, my family, and I hope I make you just as proud of me!

The book title was inspired by a song by the band White Zombie. The song name is "Super Charger Heaven" and can be found on the album named "Astro-Creep: 2000" from the year 1995. (the "Devil Man" song)

The chapter names were inspired by the song titles listed below, in order by chapter number: (listed as - song name, song album, song artist)

Chapter 1, Coming Undone, See You On The Other Side, KORN
Chapter 2, Running Down A Dream, Full Moon Fever, Tom Petty
Chapter 3, Highway To Hell, Highway To Hell, AC/DC
Chapter 4, It's Not My Time, Self-Titled Album, 3 Doors Down
Chapter 5, I Will Not Bow, Dear Agony, Breaking Benjamin
Chapter 6, Last Resort, Infest, Papa Roach
Chapter 7, The Reason, The Reason, Hoobastank

Table of Contents

Chapter One: Coming Undone 1

Chapter Two: Running Down A Dream 28

Chapter Three: Highway To Hell 37

Chapter Four: It's Not My Time 52

Chapter Five: I Will Not Bow 76

Chapter Six: Last Resort 110

Chapter Seven: The Reason 135

CHAPTER ONE
Coming Undone

"...since I was young, I tasted sorrow on my tongue..."
"Coming Undone" **by KORN, 2005**

My entire life has been an interplay of complex factors. It's like good and evil swarming all around me and battling for control of what's next. As I became mature and understood these complex factors a little better, I learned of a supposed law of nature that seemed to creep into everything that I would set out to do or accomplish. This law is known as "Murphy's Law". It states, to the effect, that anything that can go wrong, will go wrong. This unhinged story couldn't exist without the influence of this natural phenomenon.

When I pay attention to what's going on in the world, it's easy for me to notice that there are lots of unstable people everywhere. I find that most of the drivers on the road now act as if they're stark raving mad! I should know what "crazy" means because I too am certifiably sick in the head! It takes one to know one, as they say. Even when I look at a mirror and gaze into my own eyes, I see two windows into a lunatic fringe. As I look myself over with genuine analysis, what seems to look so strong, is so delicate. These eyes have seen way more than anyone should have to see. It's all my past experiences and twisted history that defines my growing lunacy! My reflection seems to have filled in with signs of wisdom over time. I spent a huge part of my life not seeing any substance to myself and wasn't able to see who or what I really was. When I was a young man, I could see the reflection of my face, but I would see all the way through myself as if I wasn't quite there yet. I knew there was more to myself than was being seen by my own eyes. I knew there was more going on around me than I could imagine. I also felt as if more things were going on around me than I was willing to believe.

When I was a teenager, I would sometimes find some satisfaction from pretending that my birth mom was a witch who was burned alive at the stake for all the sins and crimes she committed. The worst of these sins were the things she had done to me and my siblings! She was a cold, selfish, empty shell of a mother who was never there for me and therefore thankless for all the many tears I cried for her! She was supposed to be my guardian angel but instead was a dark winged evil purveyor of sorrow and sadness for me. A true bitch in every sense of the word! What causes a person to think these kinds of thoughts? Is this normal? Probably not to most people, but it was for me. Later on in life, as I sat next to my birth mom's hospital bed as she lay dying of liver failure, I had my first experience with humility and forgiveness. I hated to see her or anybody going through that kind of death, but I couldn't seem to cry. I had put the past with her behind me the best that I could, but inside my head, I knew she was paying the price for her wickedness and many addictions. I had cried myself empty of tears when I was just a little boy. Where was she then? Where was she when I got sick as a kid? Where was she when I was scared? Where was she when I needed to be loved? Where was she when I was hungry and cold? The truth be told, I probably would not be alive if abortion was legal in 1968/1969! She was very lucky that I was even there beside her on that day! As she was nearing her final moments being alive, I felt as if I were sensing unseen influences from another dimension for the first time and what I was sensing felt like a gathering of dark shadowy entities! The darkness from this other dimension was absorbing all the good light that was left in the hospital room! The ground trembled and shook for me as she took her last breath. I felt the dark forces disappear and the room quickly seemed void of the evil buzz that had permeated it just moments before. I suddenly felt enlightened and had some relief. I'm not sure if I should feel guilty about that relief, but it was overwhelming and powerful for me. Finally, I could move on emotionally and not have anger and resentment pinned up inside me anymore.

There were additional reasons for my twisted fantasies of witchcraft and punishment for my mom. One of the biggest reasons was that it provided me with a rational explanation for some of my abnormal skills. I had a number of things happening in my childhood that seemed magical and even unbelievable to me. These unusual powers defied my own logic and left me scared to even talk about them to anybody else. I eventually solved the enigma in my own head by rationalizing that these powers were passed on to me by my evil mother! That is where the most satisfaction came for me when thinking those diabolical thoughts. I will give you three good examples of the weird, almost magical occurrences that had me so concerned and confused as a child.

The first time I noticed my odd abilities was when I was around eight or nine years old. I had gotten a cheap toy from the store when we were shopping one sunny afternoon. This toy was a propeller disc launcher that sent the propeller discs up in the air about fifty to eighty feet. When one of these discs went over my house and landed in the back yard, I couldn't find the disc anywhere. I looked and looked and eventually gave up looking and was at a loss as to where the disc could have gone. Later that night as I was asleep and dreaming, I dreamed that I floated up out of bed, through my ceiling and roof, and above my house and neighborhood. I could move in any direction that I wanted to go and the scale of what I was seeing was like being in an airplane even though I had never flown in an airplane before. I looked down as I was above my house and could plainly see a brightly colored propeller disc wedged behind a pipe that protruded out of my parent's roof. The next day, I was playing outside and remembered my dream the night before. I decided to walk myself to a spot in the yard where I could see that pipe sticking out of the roof. To my surprise, not only was there a pipe in the exact spot I dreamed about, but there behind it laid my brightly colored propeller disc I had so desperately looked for the previous day. I was quick to realize that I must have been really flying above my house to come up with the precise details that I had dreamed about the previous night. How was this even possible? I never mentioned this to anyone out of fear and lack of understanding!

The second good example of my unusual abilities is about another dream that came to me on the evening of January 27, 1986. I dreamed that I was walking on a beach somewhere when I heard a loud noise above me. I looked up to see what appeared to be an extremely large helicopter flying by me and climbing in altitude. Suddenly, the machine exploded with a tremendous force that knocked me to the ground. As I looked up at the fiery explosion in fear, I saw debris falling from the sky towards me. This debris was on fire and smoke trails followed each piece as they plunged downward towards me from above. I was definitely overcome with horror at the loss of life that I had just witnessed! I became so panic stricken about being hit by the burning fallout that I hopped to my feet to run as fast as I could when I suddenly woke up in a massive sweat! I sat up in bed as I felt like the dream was more than real to me. I was unable to go back to sleep for a while as I couldn't shake the sorrow of what I had just dreamed about. I eventually was able to put the thoughts aside and go back to sleep. The next day, I walked by the television sometime in the afternoon and was punched in the gut by what I was seeing. I was having to relive my dream in real life as I watched in horror and sadness as the Space Shuttle Challenger blew up shortly after liftoff from Cape Canaveral Florida. Every detail that was playing out over and over on the television was exactly like my dream the previous night. I felt guilty about not being able to stop the event from happening. I felt cursed that I had been given a glimpse of the pending disaster just hours before it happened. *What the hell is going on with me*, was what I asked myself for the next few months. Was this ability a curse or a gift? How was this even possible for me? Why was this possible for me?

Finally, out of all the many examples I could share about my strange abilities, this example is one of the most bizarre and doesn't involve a dream. One day I got angry and shouted out loudly as I punched my finger towards a hallway in the house, pointing at it. I was shouting the word "bullshit". At that exact moment, the light bulb in the ceiling fixture that was in the hallway I was pointing at, exploded in a dramatic fashion. Sparks and glass flew everywhere as if there was a firecracker exploding inside of it! I have never seen a bulb do this in my life before or after this incident. I was so intimidated and scared when this happened that I forgot about being angry. Silence immediately followed the bulb detonation as everyone in the room couldn't believe what had just happened. I once again questioned myself and how I was able to do that stuff! What was causing me to unwillingly be a witchy kind of guy? Why was I being subjected to these seemingly magical abilities?

My name is Terry G. I was born in the spring of 1969. I lived as Terry for the first seven years of my existence. Due to my adoption at the age of 7, my full name was completely changed. It's easy for me to remember feeling weird about having to reboot my identity as someone new, especially at that age. I certainly felt real value in this new family, new name, and my new hope. I felt like a new little man! The thing is, Terry didn't go away from me, and he was always in the background, quietly paying attention. Terry must have been written into my DNA from the very beginning, just like evil was written into my DNA by my drug addicted birth parents. As I adjusted to my new identity as a kid, I always had Terry peering out from behind me, looking around. He was always trying to see what kind of stuff the new guy had going on. Terry was curious, of course! Terry was my real connection to my earliest memories, both good and bad. I always felt as if Terry represented the sadness and hardship that was, and still is residing inside of me. Because of my horrible childhood memories, I have tried really hard to always be good and kind to others even thought I felt as if I were pre-programmed not to be. It seems to me; I must be loaded with "bad-boy" style genes! *Blame Terry* is what I always think to myself. I really ought to be sharing some of the blame with Murphy and his stupid law!

Terry G wasn't conceived out of love, kindness, planning, and adoration for new life. I was a product of lust and hardcore sin in action. I was just an accident that occurred while my parents were indulged in full scaled, self-serving activities of the flesh while being drugged up and immoral with one thing on their mind, shoot to thrill! The maternal vessel that brought me into this life was powered by nothing but evil! Does that make me evil too? I can't be sure if I am or not, but I have wondered that very thing quite often. I do try to consider everything possible to explain why my continual battles over good and bad are always accompanied by weird extremes. I am talking about crazy extremes! This memoir just happens to be a story about the most extreme, and the most bizarre circumstance I have ever encountered – and a stranger who is pure evil, from his skin, all the way to his bones! I was just eccentric and twisted my whole life but now maybe I am all the way crazy!

It has gotten really difficult to mentally keep track of everything that has contributed to my loss of sanity. This book was an effort for me to organize and track my memories and provide myself with a better understanding of everything that led up to my feelings of mental anguish and loss. I needed accuracy in what I was writing to capture my life-changing encounter in 2014. I felt as if all of the details and thoughts in written form could help my efforts in dealing with it all. As it turns out, I was one hundred percent correct in that assumption!

You will notice that there are seven chapters in this book. This is no coincidence. The seven chapters represent the seven years of hell I went through after all the trauma that consumed me while traveling on route 66. Seven years of hiding from my own thoughts and trying to make the memories just go away. I live now in Las Vegas, NV where three "7's" are a jackpot. I had lived seven years as Terry, I had seven years of hell and hiding after my fateful journey, and now I have put all of my story neatly into seven chapters for this book. That makes three "7's" so let's see where it all goes from here.

There are times in my life when I feel overwhelmed by bad luck or bad influences. My fight to stay on the good side of things is complicated by these negative influences. Sometimes it is like hell's bells begin loudly ringing all around me. Dozens of loud bells all gonging my head like a bad dream. The vibrations from these bells from hell are still reverberating in me even to this day. I will share with you a few of the most influential negative moments in my life that shaped my personality, and which led me to multiple rendezvous with evil throughout my personal endeavors.

Let me start with my earliest childhood memory involving hells bells and the loud chaos that followed its intrusion into my young, peaceful world. My earliest memories are of me with my little brother Timothy (Tim). He was exactly a year younger than I was. My very first recollection as a young child is of Timothy and I being inside a dark daycare. It was an old house that was converted into a daycare at some point. Tim and I were laying on blankets on the living room floor at night, in the dark, by ourselves. I vividly remember not feeling good at all. This was because we were both sick with chickenpox. There must have been an adult there with us, but I can't recall anyone else being there besides Tim and me. We were evidentially waiting for someone from child protective services to come pick us up. There was a severe thunderstorm with heavy rain beating down on the roof and windows, and bright bolts of lightning were filling the room with flashes and shadows! We needed our mommy really bad! Scary bursts of loud thunder were making me super nervous and very scared. I couldn't help but notice that Tim was screaming and crying. And with my being raised to feel as if I were his caretaker, I was usually occupied with soothing him. What's crazy and sad is that I was about 3 years old, and Tim was about 2 years old, and I had come to feel like I was responsible for him. Tim had also come to rely on me to help and comfort him.

I took it upon myself to try to calm him at that time because, in my memory, nobody had come around to calm us. I remember getting Tim quiet for a moment by trying to teach him how to tie a shoe, even though I barely knew how to tie a shoe myself. I guess I was learning to be a problem solver, or maybe I was just trying anything I could to make him calm down. All I know is that he stopped crying and tried to learn how to tie his shoe. Somehow my efforts had worked quite well. He was temporarily quiet and occupied. Hurray! I also remember that he eventually started up his screaming and crying again. I thought maybe he needed some food because I knew that I sure did.

Nervously, I started walking around, in the dark, trying to find us something to eat. I made my way towards the kitchen. I remember opening cabinets. I remember opening the dishwasher and remember the smell of the chlorine on the dishes in the dishwasher. I remember opening drawers too and inside one of the drawers was a bag of funny shaped crackers. You know, oyster crackers, as I found out later in life. Oyster crackers were all I was able to find. So, I took them to the living room to share with my little brother. And for that moment, he was content, happy, and most importantly, he stopped crying! I remember vividly that both of us had enjoyed the snack and I believe we ate the whole package of crackers. I know I felt proud to be caring for my baby brother! I enjoyed knowing Timmy was taken care of and fed by me, his loving, older brother!

Later in life I was able to read court documents regarding that night. As it turns out, that was the second time we had been left there by our parents. This had been the second time we had stayed all night at this day care. My birth mom admitted later in life to me that she was too messed up on heroin to come and get us. Like that was going to make things any better for me! Tim and I were then forced in and out of foster care for the next few years and each time, we would be separated from one another while in foster care families. Way too many times we were separated and then reunited and then separated and reunited. It was very crazy and confusing for both of us. I don't have recollection of everything, but I do know that he clung to me, and I also clung to him. Since I was the older brother, I naturally was protective of him. It was kind of like the blind leading the blind. One thing was certain, he looked for me to give him direction and keep him safe and I never did let him down. We were forging and building lasting connections to one another, at early childhood, that would carry with us for the rest of our lives. All these personal connections with each other were very important, in fact, it was great that we had each other. There was one major complication for us. Murphy's Law begins its assault on me and Tim once again. At that time, the courts did not view things the way they should have. There were probably some individuals within the court system that would have liked to have seen things turn out differently for us two brothers but that didn't matter in our case. I understand that there were no provisions for any exceptions to the state rules regarding protective custody of minors. My adopted parents said all the conditions and procedures were frustrating. They tried to get both of us boys together, but the state rule was that each child placed in foster care must have their own bedrooms. What a shame huh?

My foster parents (later adoptive parents) had a 3-bedroom house with 3 daughters already. My parents had one room, there was a room set aside for me, and my 3 sisters were required to share a bedroom (technically). The state thought it was okay for the foster household siblings to share a room, but Tim and I had to be torn apart and not allowed to share a room. Hells Bells! Because of the wrinkles in the laws, my foster parents were only allowed to have one of us two brothers. Tim's foster parents were bound by the same problem and rules. The courts never took our feelings, needs, fears and desires into consideration. The courts that were supposed to protect us failed us in many ways. Ultimately, crazy, and horrible results came out of all the chaos for Tim and me. All the legal decisions and court actions caused us to permanently be separated from each other when we were just 6 and 7. Yep, that was Murphy chopping away at my sanity right then and there! Being separated from each other would mean that our relationship, our visitations with each other, all our communications and connections would no longer exist for us. We never had a proper goodbye! I remember the last supervised visit that Tim and I had with each other. It was in a conference room of a children's home that was located in northeastern Oklahoma. I recall Timothy and I just crying our eyes out when the visit was over. I promised him that I would see him real soon. I told him we would play cops and robbers again which we loved to do together. I had no idea how wrong I was about that. I felt guilty my whole life for making that promise to him. I wouldn't see him again for another 22 years and under severely different circumstances.

As I focused on knowledge and success in my early adult life, I was able to take my education, interests, and my skills and turn them into a great career. Once again, Murphy's Law and the annoyingly loud bells from hell would make a dramatic appearance in my life. In 1996, at the age of 27, I was in the middle of building this new successful career. It was early in my marriage, and we had our first child, and everything was perfect for me and my wife. Shortly after we had bought our first house, I received some news that was both exhilarating and incredibly scary at the same time. This news would be full of twists and turns for me and even had a second revelation that I was not expecting at all! One bright sunny day, late in the morning, I received a message regarding a phone call from my dad. I found a payphone (remember those?) that could be accessed while sitting inside my pickup truck and called him. He had a message for me and another phone number for me to call. He said that in all likelihood, I should prepare myself for some possibly shocking news. He said he honestly didn't know any of the details but figured it must be important and could be difficult for me. After hanging up the phone and taking three deep breaths, I urgently called the number he had given to me. When I got ahold of the person that was trying to contact me, that person asked me if I was sitting down. As it happens, I was already sitting down inside my truck, so I asked them to continue. I told them that I was ready for whatever it was that they needed to tell me. You know, I could have lived two or three lifetimes and still would have not been able to prepare for the news that I was about to receive. I could never have been prepared for the chain of events that followed the news and the ways it dramatically affected me throughout my life thereafter. Yeah, Murphy has been working behind the scenes for me and is now about to uncloak its unseen influences on me and my life. Evil is about to bare down on me from unexpected places and will tear at my soul and mind forever thereafter. This phone call spun my head and emotions all over the spectrum. With this phone conversation, I was indirectly provided answers to all my hidden fears and questions about little Timmy. Yes, my brother Tim was most definitely alive. However, my worries about Tim not doing very well got confirmed! A lifetime of daily sadness and anxiety for me was justified in this one phone call! This was because I found out that Tim developed issues and problems in his adopted family life. He had disconnected from his new family and society and was not doing well at all! He found himself in jail at the young, tender age of 16 years old. Then later he was in incarcerated in prison. He had turned to a life of crime as a way of escaping his misery. He was pissed off and trusted no one! I was told that he was again on trial after being in prison for many years already. I was regretfully informed that my little brother Timmy was on trial for capital murder!

One year earlier, Tim had gotten into a fight with his cellmate, and he had won this fight. Most of the time, to win a fight in prison means the other person dies! Especially if the fight is between two cell mates. This fight was no exception and my brother had now taken the life of another human being. I was told the State of Oklahoma was seeking the death penalty! I was told that my brother's defense team needed my help if possible.

The Oklahoma Indigent Defense System was representing Tim in his trial, and they were the ones who had contacted me. They were wanting to put me in touch with Tim, and the rest of our biological family, if I so desired. They made it clear that I did not have to do any of this. They told me that if I didn't want to continue, then I would never hear from them again. They made it clear to me that I was not obligated in any way and my privacy would be kept intact. It was also made clear to me that they had high hopes to be able to convince me to be interested in all of this. They thought my help would be extremely important for the outcome in Tim's trial. Of course, I began wondering how could they need my help? What could I possibly do to help Tim in his trial? I had not seen him since I was 6 or 7 years old! I was given further explanation that my brother Tim, sadly, was more than likely going to have a conviction. They said the trial was likely a clear-cut case for the prosecutor and that the death penalty was possible if my brother was indeed convicted. I was told that the possibility of death by lethal injection was the only reason why the Oklahoma Indigent

Defense System was taking his case, to save him from execution! I was told that I would be helpful in the sentencing phase of the trial to try to spare his life. My testimony would be especially important in establishing some insight into his background and maybe some insight into his behaviors and why. I needed to shed light on how and why it was important to keep him alive! Especially now that we have been reunited. Wow, no pressure, right? All of this was piling up on me while I was sitting on a payphone inside the cab of my pickup truck. Unbelievable! I am glad that I was actually sitting down when this conversation began!

I was shaking and sweating by the end of the phone call! I didn't know how to feel about all of this! I was overwhelmed with thought and emotion and wondered if I was even going to be able to finish out my workday. I immediately knew what I should do. I accepted the offer to testify in Tim's trial! I wanted to help his defense team in whatever capacity I could. It was about time that I found out about my past and the people associated with it. I needed to see Tim as soon as possible!

I was told that Tim wasn't the only brother I had. Being made aware of another brother is the revelational twist I had mentioned earlier. John K. is his name. He is nearly two years older than I am and it turns out that he knew about Tim and me his whole life. There is also a half-sister named Lisa. We all share the same mother. Tim and I had a small, limited number of memories of Lisa however, we did not know about John, at least not up until this point. This was a major shock to both Tim and me. I suddenly found that after thinking I was the oldest brother all this time, now I find out that I am a little brother. A middle brother I guess. *Wow, I have an older brother now!* I was thinking to myself. I was overwhelmed by the news. I can't put into words all the emotions that flooded me on that day. Most were new emotions to me and strong emotions too. I did notice a familiarity to a small portion of these emotions. I was completely confused but happy to sort out my thoughts and feelings about all my newfound layers to my life.

It wasn't long and lots of memory triggers began to occur as information in the form of documents and pictures began arriving at my house for me to absorb. Many more memory triggers were unleashed when actual in-person reunions began to happen. I met a huge number of people that were related to me biologically, and I also met people who were friends of biological family members. You know with most of these folks, I did not know anything about who they were, but they usually seemed to know who I was. I felt like I was being analyzed and observed by these new people. I was somewhat happy, but for a while, I stayed in a state of shock. As soon as I would feel elated about all the newness of things, the sadness and grief of what caused all of this to happen would displace my happiness and flood my consciousness and weigh me down. I still have trouble comprehending how I was able to receive the massive amounts of new information and all the new people that suddenly rained down on me. Finding out lots of the things associated with my biological family members made understanding my own personality traits possible. I also needed to learn about myself in biological areas and learn my genetic characteristics. I needed to begin to form an overall picture of myself that included my family's health history and any health issues that might affect me. I always recognized early in life that I had desires and thoughts that none of my adopted family seemed to have. I felt this was due to the biological differences between us.

I guess I should repeat that none of this reunion stuff would have even happened without my little brother Tim being on trial for capital murder with the death penalty as a possible outcome! It was because of the dire situation with him that so many people were connected and stirred up together.

What a crazy and bizarre chapter in my life!!

Again, I am subjected to extreme good and bad happening in my life at the same time, as usual. This pattern will repeat itself again and again throughout my life.

It was relayed to me that the prison officials and his defense team noted a dramatic difference in Tim's disposition and attitude after being put in touch with me and the rest of the biological family. He had a reason to live now and was surrounded with people that not only cared about him, but I personally longed for him all those years!

Tim and I had an unimaginably large amount of catching up to do. We laughed, cried, dreamed together, supported each other's shortcomings, inquired into each other's interests and childhood events, and wished the whole time we had more time during visitations to make the process easier. Letters helped us but could not replace one-on-one contact. It was like I was looking at myself in the mirror with him. We had similar facial traits. We had the same hand gestures. We laughed and giggled just alike too. Everything about Tim was so familiar to me. Everything about Tim was comforting to me. I know those feelings were just what I needed. I had no way to imagine much of those feelings until they began to occur. I figured out once again that what I had been missing, in simple terms, was my little brother!

When the time came for Tim's trial, arrangements were made to bring family members together for the defense team to use if necessary and to be Tim's support group. He was so happy to meet and correspond with all of the biological family. I recall, just before Tim's trial, I decided to call my older brother John for the first time. We would be meeting each other soon so I wanted to reach out to him by phone first. I was nervous but also excited and curious. I really didn't know how I was supposed to feel. I dialed the number as my wife quietly watched in the distance with anticipation. John happened to answer on the other end, and I had no idea who I was talking to when he said hello. I asked if John was there. He said, "this is John, is this my brother?" When I responded with yes, he got excited and said he knew when the phone rang that it was his brother on the other end.

He was surprised and happy to hear from me. We talked for a while and began the process of getting to know each other but it was awkward, and we both wished the reunion wasn't under such horrible circumstances.

Another vivid memory I have about reuniting with biological family members takes place at the airport with my wife present. An odd and nervous reunion was about to occur on that day. I remember when the airline flight arrived bringing my birth mother and half-sister. My wife and I watched out the terminal's windows as each person exited the little commuter plane onto the roll away stairs. I wasn't sure how I felt about seeing my birth mom, but I was excited to see my half-sister Lisa! My wife and I stood there trying to guess which passengers might be them as they appeared one by one in the doorway of the small turboprop plane. It seemed like the entire plane emptied before the correct people came to the door. While playing our guessing game my wife said "no, probably not them" as my sister and mom stepped through the doorway of the aircraft. It was amazing to me that as soon as I laid eyes on my biological mother's face, I intuitively knew who she was. My memories of her all went back into focus in my mind. My mind flew backwards 22 years instantly! Crazy thoughts slammed through my mind as I watched her, and sis walk across the tarmac towards the terminal door. I was nervous as hell and felt really sick to my stomach but had no idea why.

Just at that moment, I clearly remembered a time when my biological mom had run into a convenience store and left Timothy and I in her black 1970's Chevrolet Chevelle SS while it was running. She should have known that Murphy's Law was ruling her life by then, you'd think! I guess the safety devices on modern cars had not been implemented yet. One of the reasons for the safety devices being added to production cars was to prevent what happened to Tim and I. Tim had taken off his seat belt and gotten out of his booster seat and crawled up front and pulled on the gear shifter. Of course, it moved into reverse and off we went through the parking lot, over the sidewalk, off the curb, and then across the busy street in front of the store, all thanks to Murphy and Timothy. I was petrified! We hit the curb on the far side of the street, crossing four busy lanes getting there. No collisions happened, just the curb stopping the car from hitting the commercial building that was right next to it. I remembered all of this stuff because I connected her face in the doorway of that airplane with the memory of her face while she ran after us while we were barreling toward that busy street.

Tim's trial was a hard thing for me to have to endure. My adopted parents came to the trial out of respect, concern, curiosity, and to be there to support me. They knew just how delicate I was about my brother's situation. They also knew I was going to be dragged through more emotions than I ever had before. They knew that both happy and horrible feelings were on the menu for me while at the courthouse. I felt extra special to have them beside me while trying to sort out the psychological effects of this situation. Suddenly for the first time in my life I realized I was surrounded by two different families. How many people can say that?

One of the biggest pills I had to swallow was looking at my little brother and remembering the little frail baby Timmy from our childhood, while seeing a grown version of himself and knowing he took another person's life. He was still my little brother, but he was now sleeping in the bed he made for himself. I had to make myself remember that he made his own choices, and I should not feel guilty. Unfortunately, this did not completely remove my guilty feelings. I knew somehow, I needed to just focus on the positive ways that I might be able to help my brother and hope for the best.

Within days, my brother Tim was convicted of first-degree murder of another prisoner and was now waiting for the sentencing phase of his trial. I was now going to have to testify in front of the courtroom and the jury. It was time for me to find out if what I had to say could help Tim in any way. I was hoping to help but wasn't sure if I could change anything. I was nervous as hell! I answered every question with sincerity and directly from my heart. I was glad when my emotionally charged testimony was over, but I was unsure if I had any impact at all. I doubted the system at this point, and I just knew my brother would be taken away from me by lethal injection! Of course, I was shocked when the judge read aloud to the courtroom that the jury did not elect to send my brother to death row. Somehow he had escaped the death penalty! I was so relieved to hear this! When the trial was fully complete and it was late at night, I was with my brother's defense team near the Judge's chamber and the Judge asked me to come inside to speak to him. I was curious when I entered and was surprised when the judge informed me that he was told by the head juror, my testimony specifically steered them from seeking the death penalty!

Of course, I was thrilled to find out I had such an impact on the outcome! And of course, like everything in my life, it was bittersweet! As Tim's life was spared, they gave him life in prison, without the possibility of parole! The reality of all this for me was that I was only going to be able to have a relationship with my little brother through a visitor's glass and telephone.

We lived through letters and phone calls and lots of visitations and over the years I got to know my little brother like he was…my little brother! We both realized that even though it was bittersweet, it was all we had! It was all I had to connect to my long-lost little brother Tim, and I cherished every moment of it. Among many things discussed between Timothy and I, one topic of our discussions is noteworthy. On several occasions Tim had told me about his love of his life from when he was a teen. He told me that this girl was the greatest companion for him, and he insisted that she was a sexual goddess in his eyes. He even added nearly two decades to his incarceration by escaping twice to go see her! I joked with him about her being a voodoo sex girl. He always laughed at my humorous, third-party observations and comments.

One day after running his mouth to me about his days with this love goddess of his, he mentioned her name during the conversation. He said Regi**** to me. I immediately said back Regi X? His eyes got huge with a surprised look. He about choked a little when he asked, "You know Regi X"? I answered back "Oh yeah! I went to school with her." I explained that Regi X and I were in the same small class from 5th grade until 9th grade. I said I knew her extremely well. It was not long, and we both realized that we were only one person away from reconnecting to each other, all the way back in our school years. All I needed to have done is say the name of my brother in front of Regi X and she would have linked us back together. One of the disadvantages we had with reconnecting this way was that Tim was never made aware of my name changes. He never knew that I grew up under a new name.

Anyways, we were constantly exchanging wits, questions, answers, jokes, stories, good times, and everything else you would expect two "long-lost" bothers to talk about until it came to an abrupt halt in July of 2013! Murphy's Law has its most dramatic appearance! The loud piercing bells of hell turned my life upside down on this day!

Timothy, I found out one morning, had now been brutally strangled to death in prison! Murdered! I woke up one Sunday morning by a text message from our half-sister, Lisa. The continual notification going off pulled me out of my slumber. I wasn't awake yet and my groggy mind believed that this text was a joke, so I had my wife wake up and read my message. She sat up and read the message as my mind was clearing and waking up and she immediately said to me, "Oh No, honey, I don't think it's a joke"! I sat there in disbelief for a while before I accepted what I had just heard. I started calling the unauthorized, hidden cell phone that Tim had managed to get his hands on while he was in prison. He was not answering me or texting me back. I would here the ring song playing on the other end while the phone rings. He had made his song *Save Me* by the band "Shinedown". As I listened over and over to the lyrics "...Someone save me if you will, and take away, all these pills...", I felt as if it were a message to everybody. Was it because he knew he was facing a fight soon? Did he know that this would probably get him killed?

Tim was no punk. His killer had issued a death threat towards Tim on multiple occasions. Tim had a 30-year reputation to uphold in prison. He would either be ambushed and killed when he least expected it, or he could confront the psychopathic maniac like a man and be considered a hero. As it turns out, he had stood up and took his aim at the most feared man in the Oklahoma Department of Corrections. He was half the size of his killer. He was overpowered by this multi-convicted murderer and a bedsheet was wrapped around Tim's neck and pulled tight it until there was no more fight in him. The energy from the struggle and resulting murder created vibes and ripples that I could now feel, I just didn't want to feel them. I instinctively could feel that Tim was no longer with us here on Earth. I surmised that he was free from his burdens and had paid his dues to society. He had been given a life sentence. His life was over and so were his responsibilities to remain in prison. He was indeed free. Just not the way we wanted him to be.

When I eventually gave in to the fact that Tim's death had really happened, I disintegrated into a million pieces! This was an abrupt end to an amazing friendship forged out of love and out of hope.

Tim's murder broke my heart! It took the wind out of my sails! I guess they say, "You live by the sword, You die by the sword."

My mental health and stability gradually began fading. I began coming undone. My career had disintegrated for me. My relationship with my family was failing. I was looking for answers and one year after my brother's death, I finally decided to take a new lease on life! Even though I had sunken to record depths for myself and was making all the wrong choices, I pulled myself together somewhat. I had to get my act together and go back to Las Vegas where we had previously lived. I had to quickly find work. I was determined to re-establish a better way of life for myself and for my wife and kids. I had put myself and family through hell since my brother's murder. I had agreed with my wife to go there and start over while staying at her father's house who now lived in Las Vegas, NV himself. I was to prepare things so the rest of my family could follow soon thereafter. That is why I was heading on a journey in August 2014. That journey was the setting for this story.

I was by myself, of course. I was driving a pickup truck. The truck was a silver, 2000 Ford, F-150 extended cab. It had a V-8, and it was loaded down with all my belongings. You know, clothes and tools and everything that I would possibly need. I was also towing a small trailer. It was a white, low boy utility trailer. It was about 14' long and it had my motorcycle on it. I had a roll around toolbox on it and I had various things that I needed once I got to Las Vegas.

Before the trip began, I gathered up the money I needed, made my plans, and set up some job interviews for the following week in Las Vegas. As I mentioned before, I had made prior arrangements to stay with my dreaded father-in-law for a short duration. This would be only until I could start getting paychecks and find a place to rent. My father-in-law was Murphy's best friend! He was evil himself and was my nemesis! He proves to be a pivotal person in this story later. Other than the dread of my destination household, I was heading out on the highway, looking for adventure!

After I got started on this fateful adventure, events began to occur, and craziness started unfolding. It all was unexpected, quite traumatic, quite confusing, disbelieving, and bizarre. I had no idea that things were about to get worse. I thought that things in my life could only get better as I was already at the lowest point!

The circumstances that led me to begin talking about this dark time in my life was a direct result of my older biological brother John K. As you may remember, I had met good ole' John a few times when we were younger adults during the trial of our brother Tim. We had not kept in touch with one another a whole lot. He was living his life out in the Kansas City, MO area, Excelsior Springs to be exact, and I had my life in Las Vegas, NV.

Now, as fate would have it, in 2020 after the Covid-19 pandemic swept across the world, and our nation, John and I reconnected on social media and found that we were in a unique situation where I had the time off from work and he was also available with nothing going on either. He had been diagnosed with cancer and had beaten it up to that point. Without having health insurance, John was concerned about how long he would live. He feared the worst of course. We both were curious about each other's lives. After some serious discussion with my wife and kids, and careful planning, I decided to go to and get him. I would bring him back to my home and get to know him as my live-in brother and share my life with him. John and I really needed and wanted to have a working relationship with each other. We both dreamed of sharing our lives together and being able to forge new horizons together as brothers. This was incredibly important for both of us because most of our lives, neither of us had a brother around. During my trip to pick John up, I thought constantly about what this decision would do to us as brothers. I wondered how all of this would affect me and my family. I was nervous. I felt like I had an unknown destiny to fulfill by doing this. I was somehow pushed internally and driven to go get John even though I didn't really know why. I arrived and picked him up and his luggage and a few bags and then we headed west towards Las Vegas. I noticed that the uncomfortable, awkward feelings that we experienced during the first few hours of traveling together was just like the feelings I got from the "Devil Man" that I detail later. I tried hard once again to ingratiate myself to someone I really did not know.

It was like my traumatic scenario from 2014 was playing out again in some small ways. I noticed that, once again, I was stabbing westward, in a silver pick-up truck, on Route-66, with an unfamiliar person. This time, I at least knew the person a little bit and was blood related to him. However, the weird, creepiness was the theme for me for a while. Eventually, the second day, we were more relaxed and talked a little more. We were head banging to the music playing on the radio in my truck and we felt connected again with something in common. We were both unsure and nervous, but the excitement of our new brotherly relationship was foremost on our minds.

John's perspective will prove super valuable for me real soon. We were able to sit for hundreds of hours during the Covid-19 pandemic lockdown and catch up on an incredible number of things. We told stories, talked, and laughed often. We were blessed to have been able to take advantage of the situation and get to know each other.

It was during this time period together in 2020 that we were exchanging stories. I would occasionally tell him about the messed-up time I had on Route 66 with the evil guy I have been calling a "Devil Man". I was having difficulty partly because my brother looked like this "Devil Man". John also sounded like him and had a shiny knife like the "Devil Man" carried! John had a goatee and lots of tattoos just like the "Devil Man"! I would be lying if I told you that I never wondered, with humor, if my brother had actually been my nightmarish "Devil Man". I obviously knew John wasn't that guy, but the similarities were remarkable.

Unfortunately, I had mental/emotional issues when I tried to talk about this story. I told him that my main issue was Post Traumatic Stress Disorder (PTSD). I explained that I was never able to really talk about it to anybody nor did I want to. Somehow with the help of time, little-by-little, I got more comfortable with my brother. I felt a little more at ease with him and gradually began telling him some of the unbelievable details.

So now as the details began to come out, I started getting emotional! I would find myself, at times, feeling incredibly angry and I would be pacing the floor as I recalled the events and spoke about them out loud. I would get anxious. I would get tears in my eyes at times. I would be shaking uncontrollably sometimes as I spoke about what had happened. I would be oddly happy and elated at times too! I couldn't understand why I was having these feelings. As I started telling John my story, oftentimes I would have to stop in the middle of a particular detail. I would tell him that I was unable to continue telling the story. I would acknowledge that re-living the events were working me up too much. Each time, the story would come to an abrupt halt, disappointing my brother. My story had become like a reality-based soap opera for him at this point.

Somewhere along the way, my brother John noticed just how much there was to this story. He said that it was obvious that I needed to get it all out of me. He saw that it had taken place way too long ago for me to be holding it all up inside me. He thought that somehow, he had to find a way to get me to speak and clear it all out of me. He hoped that somehow I would document it all as well. He said he figured that having it written down would help me see the bigger picture. He thought it would help me understand everything much better and with better clarity. He got me thinking!

One day, after lots of careful thought and consideration about some of John's reasons for why I should write this story down. I took that bit of the new perspective from my older brother and figured he was right! I decided I was now going to take all that negative energy and the repressed thoughts and feelings and get it all out of me! Writing this down would not only make me feel much better, the story and events would rattle people to their bones, just like they did to me! I could use this story as a focal point to make my life much better. John said that I could use the story to empower myself to help others through their bad situations. He said I could be happy again if I wanted to be. He was right! It was about damned time! Seven years had been long enough! I was left horrified and scared of my own shadow by the crap that I had endured. I was now on my way to revealing the horrors associated with the memories of crossing paths with a very evil man! I now was tasked to go find all of those precise memories, packed way in the back of my head, about, "Devil Man On Route 66".

Devil Man, Devil Man, CALLING....Devil Man, Running In My Head!

While I began the process of telling my story to John, there was a point where I looked up and saw a blanket folded and laying on the shelf in front of us. I pointed it out to John and said that it was a blanket that happened to be the most important blanket that I owned. It wasn't of much monetary value, but it was a gift, years earlier, from my adopted parents at Christmas time. I also explained that it being a gift was not the main reason it was so important. I then walked over to the shelf and picked up the blanket and unfolded it. As I held it up and showed it to my brother, I said, "look John, this blanket I hold here was used to save my life!" "It gave me some serenity in the middle of a storm of fear, and a whirlwind of craziness! It was my moment of silence, and it was my moment of brief sanity. It provided me with some security. It provided me warmth!" "You see", I told him, "this blanket was the only thing that I had when I escaped from that insanely evil stranger that I tried to help out." I told him that I was huddled underneath that very blanket while in the woods outside of Flagstaff, AZ. I said, "this blanket made Hells Bells a bit quieter for me that night!" I explained how it helped me be able to sleep through that night and it kept me secure. John began to get excited as he listened closely to my every word. Oh, how he wanted to hear more. He said the things that I was saying to him seemed like a good book. He insisted that I needed to continue on for his sake too!

I decided that it was best that I start from the beginning. I told him that when I left my house in 2014 to relocate myself to Las Vegas, it all was supposed to be a moment where I was pushing towards a better life. I assured him that I was supposedly climbing out of a hole in my life after falling apart when I got word that our little brother Tim had been murdered in prison! I explained that I had lost my mind and had quite literally come undone! I was acutely aware of the fact that the rest of my story was quite intense, so I warned him that it was brutal and twisted. As you might imagine, this just amplified John's interest and he was eager to hear more from me. Finally, I began narrating my story to John with precise detail, and I'm extremely glad that I did!

If it were possible to travel back in time to the point where I am just about to leave Tulsa, OK for Las Vegas, NV, I believe I would tell myself a few things.

First, I would tell myself not to stop anywhere unless there were other people around. Only stop in a safe location!

Second, I would insist that I personally make any emergency phone calls for any stranger that needs help! I should know to NEVER give my phone to a stranger!

Third, Never let a stranger inside my vehicle!

CHAPTER TWO
Running Down A Dream

*"...I rolled on, the sky grew dark,
I put the pedal down to make some time..."*
"Running Down A Dream" **by Tom Petty, 1989**

People say that "What Happens In Vegas, Stays In Vegas"
First of all, you have to make it to Las Vegas for this to apply!

The events that followed my departure from my home in Oklahoma could not have come at a worse time in my life. I was foolishly unprepared for the chain of events that were about to occur.

My story will now start up at a point where I had been driving for quite a long time. I had made a couple of stops. I had an emergency with my trailer that I had to get fixed along the way. Also, to save money, I had slept in my truck at a truck stop the previous night. I was also planning on doing this once again if I couldn't drive straight through to Las Vegas. I was used to doing this because I had driven semi-trucks for a couple of years at this point. To be quite honest, I was lollygagging around. I was delaying how soon I would arrive in Las Vegas, NV. I did not want to go see my father-in-law with whom I was planning on stay with. I felt like doom and gloom was looming over my eventual arrival at his house. I felt sick to my stomach about everything I had ahead of me. I passed this off by thinking it was just anxiety and nervousness about soon being at the father-in-law's house. I was wrong though. I was feeling those gut feelings we all get sometimes. Intuition, as I was taught. These gut feelings were about my travels to Las Vegas. I will soon find out that these gut feelings are a prelude to my fateful journey, not my arrival, as I was thinking at that time. For the previous 20+ years that I had known him and had been married to his daughter, I was never able to get along with him. This was primarily because he was a very outwardly negative person. He had created a lot of trouble for me and enjoyed doing so. I instinctively knew that trouble was usually right around the corner with him. I was in no way trying to hurry and get there to hang out with my father-in-law!

As I lollygagged along, trying to enjoy the sights along the way, I found myself just about an hour East of Albuquerque, NM. I was west bound on I-40, which is also a section shared with the famous Route 66 from Chicago, IL to Santa Monica, CA. From here on in this story, I will refer this highway as I-40/US-66. I noticed I was getting low on gas in my pickup truck. I was in the middle of nowhere. No sign of civilization here anywhere. I had just gotten out of a long construction zone. The simple fact was that I did not know how quickly I would go through the remaining gas. I was not trying to get stranded! I had never used this truck in this capacity before. When you factor in that I was pulling a trailer full of weight. I had no way of knowing what my "Miles Per Gallon" would be for sure, especially in mountainous terrain. I had planned, in advance, for this situation. I had kept a 5-gallon gas container, full of gas, in the bed of my pickup truck. Just to be on the safe side, I decided that I would pull over and put about half of the 5 gallons of spare fuel in my pickup truck's gas tank. I just wanted to ensure that I could make it to the next gas station. I then began calculating in my head where the next fuel stop was at. I also began to look for a place to just pull over, so I could put the spare gas in my truck tank. I knew it would be dark soon.

I hoped that I would have phone signal wherever I pulled over because I wanted to call my wife and family before it got too late. I knew it was probably dark back in Oklahoma by this point. I found the next exit that was available which was exit #226, not thinking about the fact that there was nothing there. Not a person was there at all. No streetlights, no buildings, no stores, nobody, and nothing was there. There was only an on and off ramp on both sides of the highway with a bridge connecting them. I believe that the exit was there to provide access to the original Route-66 pavement that paralleled the newer I-40 superhighway. I got off the highway on this exit blindly, thinking that it was simply congestion free, and was fine for what I was going to be doing. I never considered the safety aspects of my decision. That single decision was the first in a whole series of a huge mistakes for me. It ushered in the very beginning of my problems that night. I had decided, after passing through the intersection and stopping on the "on-ramp" side of the exit, that I should first call my wife. I needed to update her on what was going on. I also needed her to update her dad on my status and estimated arrival time. My ETA at Las Vegas was now later than was first anticipated. I mainly needed to talk to her because I missed her and the kids. I needed some reassurance that I was going the right direction. You know, there is always doubts. We all second guess ourselves no matter what we do. I was just trying to alleviate those doubts while on the phone with her.

I had decided to call her before I put the gas in the pickup truck. During this conversation, my 6-year-old son, Hayden, insisted on talking to me. My wife gave him her phone and could hear that he was crying. He asked me where I was at. He was telling me how much he missed me. He was genuinely concerned about when he would get to see me next. You see, we were (and still are) really close. I am with all my children. I comforted him and promised that he would get to see me real soon. I told him I would make sure of that. I assured him that I had never let him down before and he has no reason to worry. He trusted my assurances and calmed down. We chatted for a moment and then he handed the phone back to his mother. As I was talking to my wife, I never noticed that a car had pulled up behind me. I guess I was too engrossed into my conversation. I looked to my left and at my window stood a strange man looking back at me. I jumped because I was never expecting to see anybody at my window. I know he saw me jump. I was a little embarrassed. I am certain that he got a kick out of seeing me jump. It will play out in the future that he will try to make me jump some more but he doesn't succeed. So far though, I have nothing to lead me to anything but curiosity as to why he was there. I must admit that he was a little rough looking but not bad. His clothes were clean and not old and ratty. He was smiling. I noticed tattoos and a long goatee. I was complete used to people around me having a myriad skin art and tattoos on their bodies. I barely noticed his tattoos because I was so use seeing them on others.

I want to point out that I never saw the right side of his body. I probably would have been a bit alarmed if I had. From today's perspective, he was obviously hiding his right side from me the entire time we are interacting with each other. I told my wife that someone had just came up to my window and told her to hold on as I rolled my window down a few inches. I asked if I could help him with anything. He immediately said he was having car troubles. He stated he did not think the car was going much further. He asked me if he could borrow my phone to call his wife. In consideration of the fact that he was stranded, I thought to myself, *it can't hurt to let him make a call or two*. So, I told him to wait a second while I ended my call. I told my wife what the strange man had said to me. I told her that I would let this guy make a call really quick. I told her I would call her right back, not knowing I would not be able to call her again until the next morning, under completely different circumstances, and on a different phone all together. I hung up the phone call, rolled down my window, and handed my phone to the guy. Looking back on that whole situation, I probably should have told him that I would make the phone call for him and not given him my phone. We all know that hindsight is always 20-20.

It was so unfortunate that I gave him my phone right then. I had begun to pave my road ahead with bumps and potholes. I obviously was not thinking clearly! He took the phone and walked to the rear of the trailer and began to walk up the passenger side of my truck and trailer. All the while, he was hiding his right side from me, I just was not noticing it at that time. I decided to get out of my truck to see what was going on and to put the gasoline into my pickup tank. I began pouring gasoline into the side opening using a funnel and was having some difficulty with it. It turns out that I spilled a little on myself and got it on my hands. I hate the smell of gas on myself or in my vehicle when I am driving. I was noticing him using the phone but never hearing any conversation going on. I put the unused 2.5 gallons of fuel that remained in the can, back into the bed of the pickup truck. I paused a little bit to pay attention to what he was doing. I could make out that he was typing on my phone which I could only conclude he was texting someone. I began thinking to myself about how I never said he could text someone from my number. I did not have any extra time for a texting conversation. I was watching him also franticly call somebody several times and then get frustrated when no answer awaited him on the other end. I had the feeling that he was now going to delay me further and that I could get sucked into some situation where I could be set up to be taken advantage of. I overlooked the bizarre, dark mystical energy that I was feeling. The feeling of evil hovering over this guy and now me. I must have somehow missed all the obvious things. At least they are glaringly obvious now, seven years later. I never saw what was really going on. He had begun his slow, methodical takeover of control and he was learning my weaknesses.

I was thinking how I wished I had never given my phone to him now. I was complaining in my mind about the inconvenience and delays.

I tried to take back control of the situation as smoothly as I knew how. I shouted over to him. I said, "hey, are you done with my phone?" I continued with "I am in a hurry and on a time schedule." I asked him "did you get ahold of anybody, because I need to get rolling again and, well, I need my phone too." The guy answered back "well, I can give it back to you, but I still have not gotten ahold of my wife". "I keep trying though." "I should be able to reach her real soon". "Do you mind if I try a few more times first?" I remember thinking, *oh my god, here we go again! I just need to get moving along right now!* To me, I was feeling like there was an assumption on his part that I was obligated to let him at least try to reach somebody, even if it delayed me or made me uncomfortable. He was pushing his boundaries and seeing what friction I would give back in return. I was not seeing that the longer he kept my phone and delayed me out there, the more in control he felt and the more dangerous the situation was becoming. That exit was very desolate and isolated. There was a struggle inside me because I did not want to leave him stranded with his car having mechanical issues, but I wanted to leave him ASAP!

As I stood there trying to reason with him and bring this to a conclusion, I looked over at his car sitting behind my trailer. It was a white or grey, small Honda, Toyota, Nissan, or something like that. Probably mid to late 90's model. I also noticed there was a Missouri tag on the front of the car. After some more time had passed, I shouted over to him and said, "so I see you are from Missouri?" I asked him what part of Missouri he was from. He said, "I'm from Springfield." That is when I decided to begin naming the people I knew from the Joplin/Springfield area. I did not know too many people from there, but I figured it couldn't hurt to see if we happened to know the same people. Of course, we never did cross-connect the people we each knew. Out past paths probably never crossed. I was from N.E.

Oklahoma area and Joplin was a couple of hours up the freeway and then Springfield was another hour past Joplin. They share practically the exact same landscape, terrain, peoples, and customs. He seemed like somebody from my neck of the woods. I was comfortable with the fact that we talked the same talk and that he was pleasant as hell. Surprisingly, he was kind and he had manners. Aside from the uncomfortable nature of the situation, I saw nothing wrong with this guy. I genuinely wanted to help him.

It was no time at all, and he started pacing around while trying to place more calls. I took that opportunity to tell him that I needed to do something on my phone. I said that I needed to check it. He gave the phone back to me and I should have hopped into the truck and drove off, quickly. But I did not drive off. I stood there and did a brief check on my phone then I gave it back to him. I began assessing the situation and wondered if the path of least resistance would be the best approach. I just knew that I needed like hell to get going. I ask him where he was going. He replied, "I am going to Las Vegas." "I am supposed to meet my wife there because she is already there." "She got us a room and she is waiting on me." He continued, "I know she's going to be worried." I saw an opportunity for humor and said "wow, now I know why you can't get ahold of her." "She must be having a good ole time right now." "She is probably partying and gambling and forgetting to answer you." I was kidding, of course, but he didn't laugh or smile. I realized I might have gone too far. I was trying to be funny and wound-up stepping into his business. I retracted and began thinking about my options. I never realized that he could have surmised my destination by seeing the Nevada tag that was on my motorcycle on my trailer. With reluctancy, I said to him, "you know, it's kind of funny, I am going to Las Vegas too." I had all my personal stuff packed up in the truck so high it was visible through the windows. You could see my stuff in the back seat all stacked and organized. You could see stuff in the bed of the truck. You could see the stuff on the trailer. It looked as if I were in the middle of moving. I did not think of any of this. He had now told me that he was going to Las Vegas. Who knows whether that was the truth or not, but I bought it and I said to him, "Since you were going to Vegas already, and I am headed to Las Vegas, why don't I just give you a ride to the next stop?" "Or, if you are able to call and have this car towed, I can take you all the way to Las Vegas." I told him that I could drop him off at the front door of whatever hotel his wife was staying at. I thought to myself that I could use the company to keep me awake. I mentioned that if he could help out on just one tank full of fuel, that would help me greatly. He didn't say anything immediately. He was thinking about it for a bit and then said to me, "yeah dude, that will work just fine!" He assured me that he could cover one tank of gas. I told him we would be helping each other, and we both could have the best outcome by using teamwork. He said to me that he thought that would be great as he motioned to me in a thank you style of gesture. I told him to grab his bags and let us get going. He grabbed three bags out of his car and threw them in the bed of my truck. He hopped in the truck on the passenger side and adjusted his seat. He then put on his seatbelt. That is when I said, "and off we go!" I started the truck and we headed towards the on-ramp to West bound I-40/US-66. We were headed toward Albuquerque, NM and unknown to me, an evil plot had begun to come together and was there to conspire against me. It had manifested without my knowledge. It now covertly began to brew off in the distance. It was completely out of my sight, but only for a short while! I could not help but feel like I had failed myself for allowing this situation to develop right in front of me. The true tests were yet to come. I would soon be forced into re-evaluating things.

ONCE AGAIN!

If it were possible to travel back in time and I landed at the same point in time as this story is now, I believe I would tell myself a few things.

First, Buy some beef jerky and gum and leave in your pockets.

Second, It will only work if you put the gear shifter into the park position before you attempt your Hollywood style trick.

Third, When apart from the deranged guy at a stop, leave him as fast as your truck will drive!

CHAPTER THREE
Highway To Hell

"...like a wheel, gonna spin it, nobody's gonna mess me around..."
"Highway To Hell" **by AC/DC, 1979**

Some people would say that my dad would give you the shirt off of his own back. They would be correct about that. He is that kind of guy for sure. It's just that he would be practical about it. He would insist that he keep his shirt and buy you a shirt that fits you. That solves the problem in the most pragmatic way.

That's where I say you can divide up those who'd give you the shirt off their back into two categories. Some people would give you the shirt off their back so they would have an excuse to go buy themselves a new one. All while being able to boast how helpful they are to those in need. This line of thinking is very selfish in its origins. The other group of people that would give you the shirt off their back would just accommodate whatever the needs are of the person needing the shirt. This line of thought is non-selfish in its origins. So, let me remind you to be careful when you are trying to help someone out. Make sure that you are doing it for the right reasons.

As my new sidekick and I traveled west down I-40/US-66, I automatically began to feel the odd, uncomfortable, awkward, tension creeping out of every corner of my truck. It would be less than an hour before the sun was to set, and I never was completely okay with my decision to bring the stranger along with me. I knew that I had made some sort of a mistake but wasn't sure how big of a mistake. I couldn't sit comfortably now. I don't know if it was my instinct telling me I had made a wrong decision, or if I was just catching the negative vibes from him. You know, maybe it was my guardian angels and spirit guides all screaming at me like a loud charismatic preacher at a summer revival tent. I really don't know, but something was there influencing my thoughts and I wasn't listening to it at all! I guess I felt the need to take the path of least resistance now that I had someone that I didn't know, riding with me inside my personal, secure space. I felt a strong urge to rapidly ingratiate myself to this guy. You know, start a decent conversation and a personal connection that would allow us to spend the next several hours in a decent, more comfortable manner. This would make the time go by faster and fill my curiosity. I began talking to him about Missouri and the many things to do around the Springfield/Joplin area. Southern Missouri is Ozark mountain country with several lakes, and thousands of square miles of heavily wooded ground. I asked him if he had ever been to Silver Dollar City and inside the cavern systems that lie underneath Silver Dollar City. I asked him about going to the original Bass Pro Shop and Fantastic Caverns. I asked him if he had ever done all the fishing there is to do in the area or been to Table Rock Lake or Beaver Lake. Basically, I could tell that the conversations were going okay, but not as good as I was hoping they would.

    I never felt any real connection to this man as we talked while we were riding westward toward Albuquerque. I certainly felt the harsh beginnings of regret for picking up this guy. I began wondering how this would all play out. I was optimistic, as I usually am, about what was ahead. Somehow though, I felt the evil that was present in my truck. I felt the bad energy from this guy as he sat just 2 feet from me in my passenger seat. The more I tried to converse with him about random things, the more I felt as if my talking was pushing his buttons. I had a bad feeling inside me but chose, over and over, to ignore it. It was too late to second guess this situation now. I needed to focus on my surroundings and the road and get this trip over-with as soon as possible! I figured something would spark up a conversation soon. I hoped it would anyways.

It was not long, and we wound up on a conversation about the police. I can't remember how the subject changed, but he told me he had been in prison for a while. Of course, that should have been a major shocker for me! I should have seen that he was making a move on me right then. I was thinking he was just making conversation with me. I couldn't imagine that he was trying to scare me. I am certain, after years of digesting the facts, he was trying to see how I would react to what he said to me. He was still in the process of methodically taking control of the situation in small incremental steps. Everything he did from that point forward was for instilling fear and learning my weaknesses. The problem for me was that I wasn't noticing any of this. I guess that all along, I must have felt as if I were wearing an invisible shield of some sort. Just like many other confident people, I had a ridiculously false sense of ability to "control" my surroundings and awkward situations. Now I was mentally adding to this invisible shield. This was because I had two brothers that spent lots of time in prison. I felt as if we finally had common ground and something to talk about. I was glad to hear this instead of being intimidated by it like he was hoping I would be. I had stuff to share with him about my felonious, fool hearted brothers! I really thought we were on to something now. So, I told him that I had an older brother that was currently in prison and that the fact that he had also been incarcerated was no real issue with me. He seemed aggravated by that. I also shared with him about my younger brother Tim being killed in prison just a year earlier. Surprisingly, I was greeted with silence when I shared this with him. He was quiet for several minutes afterwards. I can now see that he was recalculating his plans. Evaluating what I had just told him. He was surprised, maybe shocked by my reaction, I'm sure! He was rethinking things now that I had done the opposite of what he thought that I would do. I never even asked what he was in prison for, nor did I ask about his criminal record. I figured prying into his personal life was a quick way to cause trouble or tensions between us. Besides, I really didn't want to know at that point. I somehow thought that I needed plausible deniability for some reason. One thing is for sure, his lack of emotion was extremely concerning to me on multiple levels. I was thinking, right then, that I was just being paranoid. I was looking forward to the resolution of my new-found awkward situation.

Soon we were at the next available gas station. We were just outside of the eastern edge of Albuquerque, NM. We both got out and while he went inside, I filled the gas tank with fuel. I went inside to use the restroom and came back to my truck expecting him to be there, but he wasn't. I saw his bags still in the back of my pickup and so I sat and waited for him. Obviously, this annoyed me. I had time to get gas, use the bathroom and wait for a minute or two and he wasn't back? I really should have thrown out his bags and left him there and drove off! The problem was that I looked in my glovebox and in the seat and floor for my cellphone and discovered that he had taken it with him. *Maybe I should leave him anyways?* I had pondered this for a minute or two when he suddenly opened my door and got back in with a drink in hand. Now that I think about it, I can see that I had taken way too long to decide to leave him there, and my opportunity had now vanished! It is easy to understand all of this with the help of hindsight and years to analyze it. The truth is, I wasn't comfortable just leaving someone stranded like that anyways. I guess that's why I was in this situation to begin with!

I had no idea what might be in store for me with this guy, so I thought nothing more about it for a bit. I guess a few minutes of silent time went by as we passed through the city of Albuquerque. I remember thinking that I wished I had a hotel room in Albuquerque so I could sleep and have the ability to get rid of the guy! When he did finally begin speaking, it was like a different person had stepped into my truck. I wasn't recognizing this new personality coming from the guy now! I did, however, recognize what had changed in his personality. I had seen all of this before. He was not acting aggressive or violent, just cloudy, and weird. He had transformed into a mutated, ugly soul. A person of unusual thoughts and behaviors. Guided by nothing but evilness and wickedness. The simple fact here was that I had been born at night, but it wasn't that night! You know I could just tell by his new sudden renewal of energy, the louder volume in his voice, his eagerness to get moving down the road, and his quick movements with his hands, arms, head, and mouth, that he had just pushed a few CC's of methamphetamine into his veins while I waited for him at the gas station. *What an asshole,* I thought! He was now dancing around a ring of fire! He was calling out to the dark forces to align and assist him in bringing me into peril. He was opening himself up to the spirit world of evil and darkness. I had no way of knowing just how dark the pact was with the diabolical, Yet!

    I knew in the back of my head that this situation would probably not turn out the greatest. Foolishly, I thought I could still handle the situation though. Maybe the fact that he would be awake would help me stay awake! I was getting extremely tired and sleepy. Maybe his being weird would keep me awake while I drove the rest of the way through New Mexico, Arizona, then through southern Nevada. I can see now that I was only taking the path of least resistance some more and had no real backup plan. I had no history or point of reference by which to draw upon to guide me through this weird and increasingly scary situation. I decided to ponder some strategic scenarios while I drove, but I still never felt my life was in danger yet. I can say that I was increasingly regretful of my decision to allow him to travel with me.

We talked a little about drugs as he must have felt like drugs were his subject of expertise. I did wonder why his interest in, and my knowledge of elicit intoxicants was even of interest to him. I was looking for purpose in his conversations. I went along with this for a while because it passed the time. I was never comfortable with this line of communication with a stranger, especially him! I was creeped out by this guy now and this topic was toxic to me. I hoped for something to change so I would not have to endure this conversation with him anymore. It got to the point that I was sick of talking about the subject. I got some moments of silence to ponder things, but he always came up with more to say or ask about drugs. I knew I had a weird, deranged guy on my hands now who was not acting like the person I had picked up earlier. I now only wished for this to get over with.

I sure wasn't thinking that things would get any worse. After all, I was the guy that reached out and helped somebody. Good things come to those who take chances and help other people, right? I genuinely relied on this to be true. But, you know, it didn't work out that way for me at all. The more I tried to reason into my brain some sane purpose for all of this, the more I kept getting negative thoughts, the feeling of hopelessness and no way out. I was now constantly trying to think of ways to put all of this to an end. Mainly because I was so uncomfortable with this guy! I was obviously weighed down by sensing the evil band of demons that were now looming in my truck. I also felt the evil presence that hovered above us as we moved along the highway in the darkness of night.

It wasn't very long, and I began realizing that he wasn't handing my phone back to me. I chose not to say anything at that point in time, in keeping with "the path of least resistance" idea. A moment of silence filled the truck for a few minutes. Suddenly, my phone burst into action when my father decided to call and check on me. The guy handed me my phone and I answered it. My dad greeted me and said he was just checking on me and seeing how things were going for me. I told him that I was in the middle of an awkward situation and that I would call him back. I told him that I couldn't talk right at that moment. My dad said okay and to call him back as soon as I could. I wondered if I hadn't missed another opportunity to bring all of this to an end, but I also didn't want him to worry. I also didn't want this guy to hear my concerns about him while talking to my dad. I also didn't want him to hear my dad's reaction to said conversation. So, I figured that I had made the right decision not to say anything. Another part of me was still saying, once again, that I was just being paranoid and that all was going to work out just fine. I really convinced myself of that because as far as I could see, it all should be over with in about eight more hours. I just hated to pretend to like someone for that long when I could not stand him at all! That was the extent of my worries right then. No thought yet about life threatening danger. I just knew I would feel much better when we would eventually go our separate ways. I was operating under the assumption that I was just eliminating one worry for this guy regarding getting to Vegas to be with his wife. Which, by the way, he had not called her his wife since picking him up by his stranded car. He was only referring to her as his "girl" now. That Figures Huh? I really thought I was helping him out here!

I recall him saying to me at one point that I was driving terribly and to keep it steady to avoid being pulled over. He seemed aggravated as he verbally corrected my driving. Of course, this made me even more uncomfortable. That is when I pointed out that we were pulling a trailer in wind blowing from the side. I said the crosswind causes the truck to feel like it's drifting from side to side, but actually, it was only the trailer being pushed around in the wind. He didn't agree and said that he thought that I was falling asleep. I disagreed with him because I wasn't falling asleep…yet! However, I knew it wouldn't be long before I was dozing off. He eventually suggested to me that he had something that would help keep me awake. I knew what he had in mind, and I refused – politely though! I hoped that I hadn't in some way offended or angered him by this. I was not sure of how he would react to anything I had to say. All I knew is I did not like him, I did not trust him in any way, and I wanted to be done with him, right then! The road I was traveling was way too long and way too desolate and dark to have an evil, creepy, slimeball hanging out with me! Well, guess what? I was stuck with him.

We pressed on and it wasn't long before I did begin dozing off while I was driving. I tried so hard to keep from doing this, but every time I tried to not doze off, I would fail. I would blank out and then the next thing I knew, I was waking up moments after dozing off and feeling so scared about it. I told him that I was going to have to pull off the highway for a little bit and rest, so I wouldn't fall asleep and get us both killed in a crash. I found the next exit which had a truck stop at it and pulled into the parking lot and laid back with my eyes closed. I naturally began to assess the situation and realized that my normal routine of napping for a couple of hours was not in my best interest. In fact, I realized that just having my eyes closed could spell trouble for me. I opened my eyes quickly and sat up straight in my seat. I knew that maybe I could have him drive but that would have to be the last resort only! I knew that I had to get moving along right then or it would be even harder to stay awake. He got out of the truck while I was sitting there and was gone for about ten minutes. I should have left him, but once again, he had taken my phone with him. *Damn the luck!* I thought to myself. I then decided to take that short opportunity to rest with my eyes closed. I was already exhausted by now. When he returned, I drove over to the gas pumps and then I went inside to get coffee, pay for gas, and use the restroom. I figured we would have enough gas to make it to Flagstaff, AZ.

You know, just 30 minutes earlier, in one of our conversations, he had revealed to me that he had been out of prison for a couple of years and that he was meeting his girl in Vegas. He said that she was facing life in prison for the manufacture of meth and was on the run. He said he was meeting her at Bally's where she had a room and together, they were going to flee the country by way of the southern border. I was nervous about being told this. I should have left him at the truck stop while I had the chance. I should have made a scene at the truck stop or secretly called the police. I should have done lots of things before I left again with this raging lunatic! I guess the idea that he was confiding in me and trusting me with this type of private information was slightly comforting to me. It must have been overwriting the fear of hearing that crazy stuff. All I could think now was that I wanted that trip to be over with, without delay!

    I pressed on for a while and as expected, I had trouble staying awake. I would nod off several times and nearly drive off the road. I had to do something different before I (we) died in a wreck. As my last resort, I decided to ask him to drive for me. This was out of desperation of course. I had no other options now. I couldn't fall asleep next to the guy while parked or I could easily be robbed or killed. All I wanted was to get to Las Vegas quickly so we could part our ways. We were 2.5 or 3 hours from Flagstaff, AZ at that point and I knew it was another 4 hours from Flagstaff to Las Vegas. Once again, I was feeling trapped as hell! This was the only option for me now without causing some sort of confrontation. So, I asked him, and he agreed to drive.

    I pulled over at the next exit and we swapped seats quickly on the side of the on-ramp. As he headed around the truck towards my door, I slid my wallet under the middle of the seat, on the hump of the floorboard under it. I got out of the truck and was confident he hadn't seen me hide it. We merged back onto the highway, and I nervously watched him take control of my truck and trailer. I was scared but soon I saw that he could drive in a straight line and seemed to be doing fine. As we make our way westward, I saw that we were well into Arizona and that's when I noticed the signage for the next exit. It was for the Hopi Travel Plaza exit where there are a couple of dinosaur statues next to the interstate. I remembered that we were near the Arizona version of Skinwalker Ranch. I couldn't believe I had remembered that fact right at that moment. I knew there was a reason for this epiphany. I felt as if it were an omen of the things to come. My gut was telling me that even though things were seeming to be okay, the shit was about to hit the fan! It also felt like the bottom was about to drop out of my world! This was a feeling I was not used to feeling and I can tell you that I don't want to ever feel it again!

Not too long thereafter, I decided to confront him about my phone. I hadn't gotten it back for a long, long time now. I wanted to see if he would give it back to me plus, I wanted to alert people of my situation by text while he was driving. I also wanted to snoop into his history and messages. Afterall, it was my phone! So, I asked him for my phone and that is actually when the shit did begin hitting the fan! He completely turned on me. As his disposition gradually became angry, mean, evil, and loud, I asked myself if things were real or not. I was thinking, *Don't tell me this guy has went psycho on me........This can't be happening.......How could this be happening.......What the hell???* I was thinking all of this very quickly as he loudly said back to me that he was never giving my phone back to me! He asserted that the phone was now his and to quit asking for it. I was shocked by this. What was I going to say that would solve this one? It seemed to me that getting into a fight about my phone with this guy while he was driving my truck wasn't smart. I just looked at him with a furious look on my face, but I didn't say a word. My heart began to race, and I began to sweat. I was filled with adrenaline and my pupils dilated as my senses went onto high sensitivity alert. With my blood pressure on the rise, I began hearing my ears start to ring. I started to reason that maybe he had lied to me about his situation with his girl/wife. I felt that he was probably the one who was on the run for meth manufacturing. He must have been the one facing a life sentence. I began to imagine that he was trying to probably push his way into an ex-girlfriend's trip to Vegas. He probably had nothing to lose. He was probably more dangerous than I could have imagined! I felt in grave danger now! I realized that he had played me till now, he had control. He had control of everything about me. He had control of my fear. He had control of my destiny. He had control of my life. He had control of every one of my possessions. The only things he didn't have control of were my brain, and my wallet! I was smart enough to have hidden that pretty good when we switched seats and I was relieved to not have it to hand over to him when he later began quizzing me about it. I told him that it was in the back seat area under all my clothes and stuff. I said I would have to get out of the truck to look in the back with the light on to find the wallet. I must have somehow been convincing because he didn't pursue it anymore. This probably saved my life; I just didn't know it yet.

You know, a person would have to be a cold, demonic, cruel, self-centered, son-of-a-bitch to be taking advantage of someone who reached out to you and helped you. There are not enough people in this world that are willing to help others as it is. I can't understand some people! I sat in disbelief as this guy was driving along and telling me that, he had now said too much to me about his situation. He began to boldly tell me how he was going to rid himself of this problem by killing me! He said he would kill me and burn me in my pickup truck and take my motorcycle on to Las Vegas, NV. He said that he had followed me and targeted me because of my motorcycle on my trailer. He said that it would be faster and save him fuel and money. He said that was why he stopped behind me back in New Mexico. He said he didn't give a fuck about me! I believed him now! I was riveted with fear now! I was so afraid that I forgot about my anger. The harsh realities of this cruel world were staring me in the face. I was pushed into a corner and wondered if I could get out of it. He had said all of this while never changing his demeanor! He was plain faced and talked with confidence and in-fact which also shocked me. How can someone tell another person such horrific things while remaining calm! I suddenly felt as if the guy had done all of this before. I felt certain that all of this was planned out by him. This was super scary and made me understand that my survival depended on me, outthinking this diabolical nightmare. I also had short moments of denial. I would think to myself, *this guy is just tripping out and just tweaking! This can't be happening to me! No Freaking Way!* I strongly felt that I did nothing to deserve this, so I began to voice my feelings aloud to him. I was pleading with him and using human nature and emotional things in my pleadings. I said to him "Hey, why do you have to kill me? Can't you just pull over and let me out? I will let you take it all with you, just let me go, please"?! He shouted back "NO! I HAVE ALREADY TOLD YOU TOO MUCH ALREADY! YOU ARE A FUCKING LIABILITY NOW! I'M NOT STUPID YOU FUCK HEAD! I WOULDN'T BE ABLE TO GET ANYWHERE AFTER YOU REPEAT EVERYTHING I TOLD YOU." I said back "No, No, If I was nice enough to pick you up and give you a ride to Las Vegas, why would I tell on you? I will let you go with my shit and later file insurance claims on all of it. Besides, I have brothers who were in prison, and I understand your situation and concerns. I wouldn't try to get in your way at all" I told him. He shouted back to me "I NEED YOU TO JUST SHUT THE FUCK UP MOTHERFUCKER! I DON'T NEED YOU TO TELL ME HOW TO RUN MY FUCKING BUSINESS! I'M THE ONE IN CONTROL YOU DUMB ASS, IN CASE YOU HAVENT NOTICED! I DONE TOLD YOU WHAT WAS GOING TO HAPPEN HERE AND THERE AIN'T A DAMN FUCKING THING YOU CAN DO ABOUT IT EITHER! YOUR FUCKING TIME IS OVER! JUST SHUT THE FUCK UP MOTHERFUCKER!"

There was a split second there where I was thinking, *Wow, just like in a scary movie!*

I was scared to death and my brain was overworked, going a thousand miles an hour right then! As I sat petrified in my seat, I remembered something I saw on television or in a movie. I remembered that I could turn off the truck with the key, pull the key out, then throw the keys out the window. This would turn off the engine, lock the steering wheel, and bring the truck to a stop. It was the perfect plan I thought. It gave me hope but I had to dig real deep for the courage to try it. I even thought to myself, *Ah-Ha! I'm a smart son-of-a-bitch!* I figured that if his plan was to kill me, this was the way to have a chance to escape. I was convinced that it would work, I just needed the strength to risk the dangers and just do it! As I was looking his way and judging when to try this, and looking at the key in the ignition switch, I then noticed why he hadn't showed me his right side that whole time. I saw that he had a big knife strapped to his right side and he had his hand beside it. Where was I going to find the courage to try this now? I didn't want to defend myself against a large knife inside the cab of my pickup truck! I realized that trying this was my only option! I started a countdown in my head with the understanding that when I got to zero, I had to make my move no matter what was happening! I had to be swift and make no mistakes then get ready to run like hell! Five, Four, Three, Two, One, then I reached over for the keys and turned them backwards as far as they would go! When I tried to pull them out, they wouldn't come out! I noticed the truck wasn't running but since the gear shifter was in drive, the key switch wouldn't go all the way into the off position and allow removal of the key. Damn! All I needed to do was shove the gear shifter into park before turning the key backwards and it would have worked. I wasn't prepared for this to fail in any way.

 Oh my God, did that piss him off! The Hollywood trick didn't work for me! I find myself in a worse situation now than I was before because now he is yelling at the top of his lungs! He slipped the gear shifter into neutral and started the engine while we were still moving down the road. He then reached for his knife and pulled it up for me to see while yelling at me. He yells to me "THAT WAS THE STUPIDIST SHIT

I HAVE EVER SEEN YOU FUCKING DUMB ASS! YOUR STUPIDITY MAKES ME LAUGH YOU FUCK FACE! NOW, I WANT YOU TO TAKE YOUR SEAT BELT OFF AND ROLL YOUR FUCKING WINDOW ALL THE WAY DOWN! AND LEAVE IT THE FUCK DOWN! IF YOU DO ANY THING ELSE THAT STUPID, I WILL ROLL THE TRUCK AND YOU WILL FLY OUT OF THE WINDOW AND DIE. I DON'T THINK YOU WANT THAT TO HAPPEN DO YOU?" He jerked on the steering wheel left and right and made the truck sway heavily and tip from side to side while we were moving along at 70 mph! This was scary as hell, and I knew he was serious. That wouldn't be all that he does though. He yelled again at me "IF YOU TRY THAT SHIT AGAIN, I'M GOING TO…" and he takes his knife and swings it, full force, in a sweep of his arm, right into my chest area. He thrusted it right where my heart is located and stopped the knife tip just a centimeter or two from my chest! I felt my shirt move a little from the tip of the knife as he finished his raging statement "MAKE SURE YOU DON'T DO ANYTHING ELSE, EVER AGAIN! THE NEXT TIME, FUCK HEAD, THE KNIFE WON'T STOP YOU MOTHERFUCKER! DON'T BE PLAYING ANY FUCKING GAMES WITH ME!" The last thing he shouted to me in that moment was, "OH MY GOD! YOU ARE FUCKING STUPID!" As it turns out, I was already thinking that very same thing! I was contemplating how my imbecilic decisions may have just put myself into "CHECK-MATE"!

ONCE AGAIN!

If it were possible to travel back in time and I landed at the same point in time as this story is now, I believe I would tell myself a few things.

First, Nothing that I have to say will stop him. Keep my mouth shut to avoid more trauma!

Second, Don't bother taking anything away from him. It will only add to his anger, and you can avoid a lot of grief by not doing it.

Third, If it's too dark to see over it, don't jump over it!

CHAPTER FOUR
It's Not My Time

*"...this life that we live is not what we have,
it's what we believe..."*
"It's Not My Time" **by 3 Doors Down, 2008**

You know that kind of trauma, it does weird things to the human body. It rewires your brain's neurological connections and changes it's chemistry. It makes the part of your brain that is responsible for the "fight-or-flight" hormones go into a state of overload. There comes a point when your body can't react with any additional resources to help you beyond what it has already reacted with. At that point you are literally paralyzed. That was exactly the condition I was in during all of this! My brain was over tasked as well! I had to call upon all the strength and will to live that I could muster up to possibly make it through all of this. I was certainly feeling things I had never felt before in my life! I was beginning to feel severe panic and I had much more yet to endure. I would live the rest of my life with the aftereffects of this hopeless situation. I guess anybody that has been in war or had something horribly traumatic occur to them would understand exactly what I am referring to. I became numb. I felt like all my senses were in overload mode as well. I had never felt this before and didn't have time to think about it right then. To be honest, sensory overload is a weak description of what I was feeling right then. It took me to a place within myself that I had no idea existed. I was filled with horror and fear beyond description. My life was flashing before my eyes. I could feel severe tingling in my hands. I could only imagine what my blood pressure was doing but the loud ringing in my ears indicated to me that it was probably at an all-time high!

Denial was the best way to convince myself that I was going to be fine. I reasoned that this guy had heard enough of my story and situation. *Surely inside him somewhere there is a heart*, I thought. I remembered that he was polite and had manners when I first met him. I felt this was because he had been raised to have those qualities instilled in him and was not just acting on his part. This could play into my strategies so I decided that I would explore that line of thinking some more. I decided to talk to him about things and see if I could break through to him somehow.

In the meantime, I really thought it was a good idea to take his advice and shut up. I would take a moment to be quiet, just as he had loudly instructed me to do, then use that time to decide what I was going say to him. I needed to decide when and how I was going to escape this situation or figure out what my options really were.

By this point I was so riddled with fear that I still couldn't move. However, I knew that I must move my right arm around to the side of the seat, towards the back seat and floorboard, and see what I could get my hand on. Maybe I could reach one of my tools like my hammer. Maybe there was a knife or something I could reach that would help me out. So, I slowly moved my hand and arm to my right trying to not move my body or be noticed. I wasn't too eager to see his big knife again, but I had to try. As I reached back behind my seat, I felt around and the first thing I felt was my motorcycle helmet. I thought to myself, *a helmet of all things! I can't even pull this through the opening between the seat and the door!* Well, I didn't think that would help me too much, so I kept probing with my hand and the only thing I came up with was my blanket that my parents had given to me a few years earlier as a Christmas present. This was the blanket I told you about earlier when I had pulled it off the shelf to show my brother John. I knew this could be handy if I could somehow escape this terroristic maniac! What I had found wasn't my jacket, but if I had to make a run for my life, a blanket seemed like a good thing to have in my hand for many reasons. I pulled it closer to the door and made sure that I could grab it quickly and easily if the opportunity arises to flee for my life.

During all of this I was constantly trying to come up with ways to help myself, even if obscure. One of these ways was when I managed to reach up with my left hand and pop the dome light cover off without being noticed. I quickly pulled the bulb out of its electrical socket and let it drop to the floor. I then put my hand and arm back next to me and was surprised that he never noticed me do this. I figured if we wound up pulled over and I was forced to find my wallet, I could use the darkness inside the cab to my advantage somehow. Even if it only gave me a little extra time, it was worth the effort.

As time slowly went by, I tried once again to use my right arm and hand to locate anything I could possibly find behind my seat. I tried hard to not be noticed, but this time my movements had gotten noticed for sure. Suddenly, he began yelling at me like a psychopathic maniac saying "WHAT THE FUCK ARE YOU DOING...MOTHERFUCKER? I'M NOT STUPID, YOU KNOW!" I quickly respond with "I'm looking for my wallet that's back behind me somewhere!" Of course, he made me stop looking for it and keep my hands where he could see them. I guess he was smart enough to realize that I was either hiding my wallet or trying to find a weapon or something to assist me. I sat there in relief that he hadn't freaked out on me just then. I was also glad that I had located my blanket and made it ready for deployment when necessary. I knew that I would not be able to prepare or search behind my seat anymore.

Adrenaline had once again filled my veins and sleep was the last thing on my mind. Desperation and fear had begun turning into analysis and a replenished will to live! I began taking account of what I had done up to that point. *Let's see, I had hidden my wallet ahead of time in a good spot. I gave him a reason why I can't just produce the wallet by lying to him about its location and explained that I would need to have the truck stopped to look for it. I had popped out the dome light so it would be dark if the doors were opened. I located my trusty blanket and made it easy to grab in a duress situation. I also have a motorcycle helmet within my reach behind my seat. Are all these things enough to help me successfully remove myself from this situation? Am I even going to get out of this situation?*

I remembered something important to me right then. I remembered how earlier in the day, I had talked to my 6-year-old son, Hayden, on the phone. I thought to myself, *Shit! I just told Hayden that it wouldn't be long before he would get to see me!* I knew in my heart that I had to survive and make good on my word to my son! It was extremely important! I began praying inside my thoughts saying, *Dear God, if you're there please help me make it through this and I promise to make things more than right!* I also thought, *Please let a higher source of power grant me some serenity and strength to overcome this!* I asked myself *What the hell is at play here?*

At some point, I focused in on the fact that it was extremely dark when driving through eastern Arizona at night! It is high elevation desert that is best known as S.W. Native American territory with a few different tribes associated there. As you travel along the dark highways there you don't see any lights. You don't see any towns or exits. You don't see any sign of life at all except the trail of lights coming at you on the opposite side of the highway. It is just dark desert. It's desolate, spooky, and huge in size. Just driving through there in any other normal circumstance invokes creepy and weird feelings. Now the feelings were downright scary as I was traveling through there in a literal ride for my life!

I shift my thoughts to the reality of; *did this son-of-a-bitch just tell me he was going to kill me and burn me in my truck?...............He damn sure did! He said he stopped behind me because he wanted my motorcycle! How stupid can I possibly be?* One thing was for sure, I was so scared, I couldn't move at all. When he thrusted that knife at my chest and it looked like it was going into my heart, I never flinched or jumped one little bit! Oh, inside me, I jumped through the roof of the truck. However, my body didn't move one inch. I know it was because I was paralyzed but for that moment in time, I had a smile inside me. I thought *That son-of-a-bitch didn't get me to jump, even when I thought that knife was headed into my chest!* Maybe calling it a smile isn't enough. I was looking for anything that was positive or gave me hope. The fact that he didn't make me jump was a small victory in a way. It was the only thing positive I could pull out of that whole scenario, and I was running with it now to help me cope in some way. It was all I could come up with. I realized right then that if I would have had a pistol, I would have filled him full of so many holes that he would have looked like a blood sprinkler as he bled out!

I couldn't believe that asshole planned on killing me! As I sat there in the darkness just 2 feet from my possible killer, I thought about my family and began to get angry and worked up! I thought to myself, *I won't let this guy kill me!.....Bullshit on him!.....I know better, deep inside of me, that it's not my time!.....Besides that, I am way smarter than this fucker by a long shot!.....As a matter of fact...* Then, right at that moment my silent thought spilled over into me verbalizing to him. I was saying loudly, "You are not going to kill me!....I am here to tell you that you may do lots of things, but I promise you, you will absolutely not be killing me tonight!"

Do you have any idea what happened next? Yeah, that's right, he wasn't going to tolerate me lashing out at him in that way! As you would expect, he screamed at the top of his lungs to me, "JUST WHO THE FUCK DO YOU THINK YOU'RE TALKING TO? I HOPE YOUR

FUCKING BRAINLESS ASS HAS BEEN SAYING YOUR PRAYERS BECAUSE THIS IS THE LAST NIGHT YOU'RE GOING TO HAVE ALIVE MOTHERFUCKER!!" It's at that point when I felt really desperate! I had gotten myself into a situation so hopeless that I am now having to beg for mercy. I had difficulty with this portion but knew it was a possible way to make progress on saving myself. So, I said to him in a mild, meek voice, "I'm serious here, and I don't want to die, nor do I deserve to die." "My family doesn't deserve this!" I told him with a little bit more volume in my voice. I continued with, "I have children that rely on me, and they love me. They need me in their life, and you don't have to prevent that this way. All I need to do is be there to provide for them and pass my experiences on to them!" I told him that I couldn't guide them if I were dead! I asked him if he couldn't do it for me, then could he spare my life for my kids? I pleaded with him, "please…..please, find it in your heart to not destroy my family's happiness and hope." I told him that I cared about him and his future too! I told him that I wished he would show me that same level of respect and consider my wife, kids, and even my… and he interrupted me screaming, "THAT PSYCHOLOGY BULLSHIT AIN'T GOING TO WORK ON ME MOTHERFUCKER! YOU DUMB FUCKING PIECE OF SHIT! I DON'T GIVE A FUCK ABOUT YOU! I DON'T GIVE A FUCK ABOUT YOUR KIDS! I DON'T GIVE A FUCK ABOUT YOUR FUCKING WIFE OR YOUR LIFE! YOU ARE GOING TO BE DEAD VERY FUCKING SOON AND IF I HEAR ANYTHING MORE OUT OF YOUR FUCKING MOUTH, I'M GOING TO"….. Right at that exact moment he took his knife and once again plunged it swiftly toward the center of my chest with full force! Once again, it stopped within an inch of penetrating my sternum and into my heart! As he flailed his weapon my direction, scaring the shit out of me again, he continued his screaming rant, "FUCKING MAKE YOU SHUT UP FOR GOOD!" He slid the large, shiny, cold blade of his survival like knife up my neck and rested it flat, up against my lower chin and held it there for about 10 seconds while I tried not to move or swallow! He said in a quieter, more sadistic tone, "I know a painful way to shut your dumb ass up!" Then, without saying anything more, he paused then removed the knife from my neck area. I concluded that I had just failed at trying to be a shrink! I had a new priority in life called "shutting the hell up!"

Even when I recall these events and then try my best to capture the moment and feelings, the words gets me worked up and emotional. It was extremely difficult to live through these things and just as difficult to write accurately about them. I get physical symptoms sometimes when I recall and write about these things and the symptoms are like the ones I felt during my horrific encounter! I get out of breath just like I did right after he did that unthinkable assault for the second time. If I remember right, I think my arms were tingling and numb, and not just my fingertips anymore. That makes twice now that I thought I was dying by a knife stab into my heart. Once again, I didn't flinch or jump! The simple fact is that I now had a high level of fear that was blocking all my other emotions right then. If I had been drinking plenty of liquids, I surely would have pissed in my pants! My brain was pushed into turbo mode once again and I had to apply some discipline and focus my racing thoughts. I knew this bullshit situation couldn't last forever. We were just going to run out of gas at some point if nothing else changed during the rest of this horrific trip. It's funny how running out of gas would be a great outcome right at that moment. That was the only time in my life that running out of gas was my primary objective. It is so ironic to say the least!

I began asking myself how I will get out of this situation. I figured I needed one good plan and then one or two more backup plans. I needed to think these things through. I knew if I stayed quiet, we had enough time before we would run out of gas to put planning and strategy into action. I asked myself what the best scenario would be. I concluded quickly that the best scenario would be that he would continue driving without interruption or angry provocation towards me. Then we could get to Flagstaff, AZ and pull into a gas station for gas. I would then run and make a scene if he was chasing me, or I could get help calling the police if he wasn't chasing me. I thought, *Boy, I hope it works out that way.* I hoped I didn't wind up getting killed trying to get some help or get anybody else hurt or killed! It was a lot to think about. I wondered if I would need to jump out of the truck before it came to a stop just to ensure my safety from him and his knife.

Shortly after that, we entered a road construction zone on the highway. The speed limit was now 45 mph and there was a semi-truck in front of us which slowed us down even more. I guess we were traveling at about 40 mph, and I imagined that I could grab that motorcycle helmet, then quickly pull it over the seat and put it on my head. I would have to open the door to the truck and hang onto it as I slowly let myself down to the pavement in a controlled fashion. I would have to hold on to the helmet straps with one hand while holding on to the door with the other hand. This sounds extreme but I was in an extreme situation with my life in the balance! It seemed much better than just jumping out of the truck without a plan. I hoped that by doing it that way, I wouldn't roll, or tumble and I could just hold on to my helmet to keep it on until I would come to a stop. *Hmm, let's think about that for a moment,* I thought! I began to conclude that maybe that wasn't such a good idea! Nothing about that plan seemed to benefit me without resulting in severe injury. I knew I would get a road rash from hell at the very least! That would have required lots of surgeries to graph skin back to the areas of my body that the skin was removed by pavement friction! No way! I would be alive but miserable and disfigured horribly! What if I didn't land correctly and I wound up tumbling anyways, breaking my neck or back? What if I accidently wound up being rolled over by the rear truck tire or the trailer? I could be knocked out cold but otherwise come to a safe stop and lay vulnerable in the road, in a construction zone, at night, with no lights, and no way for another vehicle to see me early enough to stop! Then, not enough room for it to swerve to miss me. I would then be hit and killed by a vehicle that was following us! As you can imagine, I decided against this plan all together. It was time to do some more thinking. I was thinking there was no way I was going to let this fucker kill me, so I needed to dig deeper for a different plan.

   I thought about my situation some more and figured that he was going to have to stop at some point. That was a fact! It would probably be due to needing gas. I wasn't sure if he would pull into a gas station or not. I was thinking, *surely he doesn't expect to pull into a gas station, and I will get gas and we will continue on our merry way!* He would have been crazier that I thought he was if that were the case, and he would also have been wrong! I knew he was smarter than that. I just hoped that I could somehow avoid having this fool stab or slice me up before we could even get to a gas station. I knew deep inside me that I had to prepare to seize the next available opportunity to grab my blanket and make a run for it. It seemed inevitable at this point to me. I would have to do this even if the truck wasn't completely stopped yet.

   So far, I thought to myself, *being quiet seems to be working!* I realized we had gone for about 30 minutes, and I had not heard a peep out of his ass! I honestly was using this time to just think, and think, and think! My emotions were running wild. It got to the point once again where I was questioning whether all of it is real or not. I was wondering, *was I asleep and caught in the middle of a terrible nightmare? How could this be happening to me? What in the world did I do to cause this to happen? This asshole is the one who deserves to die, not me!* He was in no way the person I thought I was helping when I asked him if he needed a ride to Las Vegas!

   I was slightly encouraged when I began remembering how I was a very fast runner while in high school. I ran cross country and I played basketball. I was in fantastic shape back then, way back in the day. Now I was required to somehow tap into that forgotten ability and run like Speedy Gonzalez! I knew I wouldn't win a fight with the jerk, especially since I had no weapons, and he had an eight-inch bladed knife at a minimum. I guessed that I needed to be ready for anything while continuing my silent observations.

As the time kept ticking at a snail's pace and the darkness rolled by into more darkness, I couldn't see anything out of my window. I was feeling very little except fear and numbness that had now spread all over my body. I started thinking about what I would do if he began stabbing or slicing on me. I wondered what I could do to defend myself. I remembered that all I had found earlier was a motorcycle helmet. I guess I could have pulled it out and hit him real hard on his head with it. But I figured that I would probably not be able to get it out and strike his head before he had stuck his knife in my arm or maybe even worse. I ascertained quickly that wasn't a good idea either. I reasoned out that if he started slashing me or stabbing me that I would have to make a jump for it out my door and hope for the best. I knew this was my final, last resort plan. I wasn't excited about this plan, but it was an option if I was defending off a brutal knife attack. Oh my god, I hoped to avoid this outcome big time!

Of course, the next two hours were the longest 2 hours, EVER! Other than the hypnotic sound of the road, it was quiet as hell. Considering the level of tension in my truck, I thought it was eerie and weirdly quiet, although I wasn't complaining. I was consumed with fear, and I prayed that he wouldn't freak out on me and attack me when we pulled over eventually. I reflected on my childhood and my achievements. I reflected on the good times I enjoyed with my family and hoped to be able to have more of them. I still had no idea where we would be pulling over and I didn't have the courage to ask him. I just had to stay quiet and wait.

Sometime in the middle of all this terror filled driving, he grabbed a cigarette out of a pack of smokes and lit it. As he exhaled the smoke slowly, he stared out of the windshield as he drove as if he was planning or thinking hard about something. I noticed that he had sat his knife down in between us while he was smoking. I immediately thought, *Guess what? You just fucked up asshole!* I slowly moved my left hand down in between us and grabbed that knife. I gripped it real hard! I felt some sort of energy from the knife as I positioned it for use. I felt very empowered and planned on shoving that damn knife into his neck putting him and all this bullshit to an end! I wanted that shit over with right then! I needed to ensure that I was not a victim of a violent, drug addicted, prick that stalked me and assaulted me! Another part of me wanted to say to him, "I got your fucking knife" and then throw it out the truck window! I had to tell myself, *Whoa, let's think about this!* I knew I wasn't ready to use that knife yet, so I moved the knife slowly over my lap. I passed it over to my right hand and gently placed it on the floor between my seat and the door. I was more comfortable knowing it was there on the floor and not in his hand. I figured it was time that I did some more thinking. Then, I asked myself, *What the hell am I going to do with this damn knife?* Remember, he had me take my seatbelt off and roll down my window! He had already drove the truck erratically, demonstrated how easy it would be to roll the truck and get me thrown from the vehicle. This would have certainly spelled instant death for me! I considered that if I stabbed or sliced him, I would wind up killing him, but then how would I maintain control of the vehicle? I considered that he could purposely roll the truck as he was dying from my attack on him. I even thought about what fresh hot blood gushing all over my hand and possibly all over me would feel like. I imagined the stench of fresh blood all over my pickup truck and me. I imagined that even if the mess could be cleaned out of my truck, I would never want to drive it again. I would also have to live with the fact that I had taken someone's life for the rest of my life. I wasn't sure if I needed to kill him, after all, he had aborted killing me twice. I was just petrified of the thought of killing another person no matter the reason. I don't know what stopped me for sure, but I am positive now that I made the right decision. I am glad I didn't kill him at that moment because my being here today and living to write about all of this proves that I didn't need to take his life! I would have been subjected to arrest, trial, and paying for a defense lawyer if I had taken his life. I would have been exonerated but I would have had an incredible amount of stressful luggage that would accompany that decision. Well, we all know that I couldn't have that happen. That would be a whole different kind of hell! I again asked myself, *what the hell am I going to do with this knife?*

My thoughts quickly changed into fleeing mode. Maybe if he didn't notice that the knife was missing, I might have an opportunity to run with my blanket and the knife! I thought that would be awesome if it turned out that way! However, a few seconds later, he reached down for his knife, and it wasn't there. Oh, my lord! I really pushed his buttons that time! I knew in a flash of thought that I was in for some drama and violence. Maybe this was it for me now. UH-OH! was what I was thinking when he burst out in a rage and screamed to me, " WHERE IN THE FUCKING HELL IS MY FUCKING KNIFE?" He begins weaving the truck left and right in a reckless manner from one lane to the next lane and back and so on. He continued screaming, "I'M GOING TO KILL BOTH OF US YOU STUPID BASTARD!... NOW, WHERE THE FUCK IS MY KNIFE?" I hesitated to answer but I knew I had no choice. I felt damn stupid having to give him his knife back. I had already weighed out the options and figured it was the safest one. I wondered if I was handing over the very weapon that would soon bring my own life to a violent end. I hoped he wouldn't kill me just for taking it in the first place! I felt this was my only shot at possible survival. So, I sucked in my pride and fear, and I told him "I'm sorry!" as I lifted the knife up from beside my seat. I handed it back to him saying "I'm sorry" again to him as if this was going to help. He grabbed the knife from me in an angry rage and flipped it over to where the blade was facing down while he held it. He quickly thrusted it towards my chest once again, and for a third time, it seemed like God had reached down from heaven and stopped that sinister knife just centimeters from my sternum and heart! He again shouted at me, "THIS IS YOUR LAST FUCKING WARNING! YOUR TIME IS DRAWING NEAR MOTHERFUCKER! YOU DID THE RIGHT THING BY GIVING MY KNIFE BACK TO ME BUT, THAT WAS A STUPID FUCKING MOVE YOU DUMB ASS SHIT HEAD! YOU ARE THE STUPIDEST MOTHERFUCKER I'VE SEEN IN A LONG TIME AND AM GOING TO ENJOY KILLING YOUR FUCKING ASS!" I guess maybe I was expecting some sort of outlash from him but, I wasn't prepared for what I had gotten from him again! But, looking back on it now, I am still sure that I did the right thing!

I was being pushed harder than I had ever been pushed. I was under severe stress, but I was able somehow to think and use logic. In the middle of all the terror I was enduring, I was able to compare my situation to the Roadrunner & the Coyote from the old cartoon series. You know, Wile E. Coyote thought he was a super genius. He was always coming up with different ways to try and catch the Roadrunner so he could eat him. He ordered various gadgets from ACME and used them to help try to catch the Roadrunner. The thing is, the Roadrunner was never caught! For one, he was extremely fast and could always get away from anything after the "Beep-Beep" sound. Secondly, he was smarter than Wile E. Coyote was and always instinctively knew what Wile E. Coyote was up to, and where he was at! I really thought that this evil guy considered himself an intelligent, sly, super genius too! He was thinking that he controlled me and my possessions. He was proud of his prowess and smarts at that point! So instead of feeling like an idiot, I decided that I had to become like the Roadrunner in all aspects. I needed to have perfect situational awareness and be prepared for his every move. Most importantly, just like the Roadrunner, I would have to time my escape perfectly and I'd need to be fast and decisive when the opportunity arose for me! Hopefully I would get the opportunity to escape! I guess I also needed to be the Roadrunner without having a bird brain too!

I once had a Bazooka bubble gum wrapper as a child that had a Bazooka Joe quote in it that has stuck with me all my life. It said, "Have an open mind, just don't let your brain fall out!" I found this to be the case on this crazy night. It was great advice for many situations including this one.

The most likely thing was that I would have to make a run for it soon. I only needed to keep or prevent this fool from cutting me up in the meantime! He was looking angry and concerned as he drove through the heavy darkness, but he was quiet, and I prayed it would stay that way! I needed to be successful at saving my life and that was all that mattered! My poor heart was racing, and it had been racing for a while. Time seemed to stretch out and seemed very slow. It was truly hell on earth for me!

This guy reeked of evil! All that was forefront in my mind was that big shiny knife of his! I kept considering how I had just handed it back to him and how that gamble could cost me my life soon. It just added to an already terrible and intense situation. The first time he had thrust the knife at my chest, I had no idea he was going to stop it. I had a second or two where I didn't know if the knife had penetrated my chest and I just hadn't felt it yet, or he had stopped it. It was when I felt the shirt that I was wearing move from the tip of the knife that I knew that I hadn't been stabbed. The psychological and physical damages had already been done even though the knife hadn't stabbed me! I can promise you that! I wondered whether he would really kill me or was he just playing games with my head. I wasn't sure of the answer to this, but I had to operate as if he meant what he said. Another thing was for sure, I wasn't saying a damn word to him!

I had been watching the fuel gage from where I sat. I knew that time was drawing near for something to happen. I knew that the next real exits available for us were in Flagstaff, AZ. That would be as far as our fuel would allow us to go anyways. I had forgotten there were a couple of exits just before Flagstaff that were isolated and empty. I was thinking that we would be forced to exit where there were other people and that would play into my favor if he didn't stop to kill me before then. To humor myself, I wanted to ask him if he was going to do his killing before dinner or afterwards. However, I just remained silent and hoped to be able to get my ass away from him!

As we slumbered along with my trailer in tow, through the darkness, we began climbing in elevation. We were on the ascent into Flagstaff where the elevation is 6000' to 7000' above sea level. I kept thinking in my head that he could just pull over anywhere, at any time, and just get violent and try to kill me. As you might remember, I hid my wallet and hadn't produced it yet. I hadn't handed any cash to him. That was ultimately what was keeping me alive at that point, I am sure of it!

Having found my blanket and making it easy to grab seemed to be an important thing for me if I were going to make a run for it. I had my window rolled all the way down, as I was previously instructed to do, and the wind was blowing directly on me. As we got higher and higher in elevation, the wind was getting colder. It was chilly as hell now and knew that in Flagstaff I would be freezing my butt off without a jacket or my blanket! Thank God for the small things is what I say! As we were gradually climbing in elevation, the overwhelming, sweet smell of pine trees filled the inside of my truck. It made me think of camping with my family and friends. I figured that I would most likely be doing a little camping that night myself. Although, the camping I would be doing that night wouldn't be the typical, sit by the fire style of camping. No hot dogs, no marshmallows, just me, hiding somewhere, under my beloved blanket! *That's all I will have,* was what I was thinking! That was a scary thought! If only he would go to an exit with a gas station. Then I could ensure that I got away from his ass, not loose all of my stuff, and hopefully not get hurt in the process!

What's next, I thought. *Maybe he wouldn't even go to an exit to stop. Hopefully I don't have to fight him on the side of the road! I just don't know!*

Hey, what was amazing was that guy hadn't said a word in quite a while. That was how I got so much of my thinking done. All of my thoughts and analysis were because he wasn't saying a word, thank God!

Man, oh man, I needed him to run out of gas or stop the truck because I was now getting cold as hell, and I needed that blanket right away! I was also thinking by this time, *if only I could have found my jacket too!* I was wishing I could have taken it along with me. The gas gage was already showing fully empty, and we were now super close to Flagstaff, AZ. I was noticing a stronger smell of pine trees in the air now. I was also shivering. We passed a couple of exits and I wondered what the guy was going to do. We approached the off ramp of exit #204 and he slowly made his way over onto it. As we were slowing down, I said to myself, *this is it! My life depends on the next 30 seconds and how I handle whatever happens.* I thought, *someone cue up the "Beep-Beep" sound effect! I am about to exit stage left, via my right passenger door! Then run for my life!*

That entire time he hadn't said a damn thing to me. I had no indication of what he was about to do. I just wanted to get the hell away from him! I knew something bad was coming because he had his knife gripped tight in his right hand. He kept looking at the gas gage over and over and then he looked over at me just as we are almost stopped. I didn't give him the satisfaction of seeing my eyes as I had other plans of my own right at that moment! Fuck him! I grabbed the door handle and as I pushed the door open with my right leg.

I grabbed my blanket from behind my seat with my right hand and then I was off in a furious flash towards the rear of the truck! I took off just like the Roadrunner. I could have beaten Speedy Gonzalez in a foot race right then! Instead of carrying cheese like Speedy would do, I was carrying my trusty ole blanket!

I had observed earlier that he had no experience with pulling a trailer as he had been driving like crap with my trailer in tow. I knew he wouldn't be able to back up the trailer without jack-knifing the whole thing so I figured I should run towards the rear of the truck if possible. That way he couldn't use the truck to back up and hit me or chase me. Yep, that was my plan and it worked. He yelled obscenities at me as I fled the truck. He tried to back up the truck and couldn't do it. I ran past the end of my trailer and went another five feet before I made a quick right turn, running past the back end of the trailer and up to the guard rail next to the road. At that point, I leaped over the guard rail not knowing what was on the other side of it. I knew there was an embankment that sloped down from the off ramp to the level of the highway. The problem was that I couldn't see anything due to the fact there were no streetlights, and it was pitch black. My luck would have it that there were sizeable rocks and small boulders covering the embankment on the other side of the guard rail. As my feet landed on these small boulders, I tripped and fell, head over feet, all the way to the bottom where I hit hard and awkwardly! I was lucky that I hadn't broken my neck or knocked myself unconscious on the way down! I had too much adrenaline in my system to feel my pain, so I leapt up to my feet and ran alongside the highway, against the westbound traffic, with my blanket in tow. I didn't know if he was following me or not. I just ran like the Roadrunner would have run.

As I saw the first vehicle approaching me on the highway, my mind instantly went into help mode. I noticed that the approaching vehicle was a semi-truck, so I stopped running and waved my arms in the air signaling that I needed help. To my surprise, the driver never even slowed down. The truck just flew by me like I wasn't even there! I then began running again in the same direction not knowing whether the asshole with the knife was chasing me or not. I did not want any more drama from him! I just wanted someone to call the police. I figured the cops were the only people that could help me at this point. I had no other plan. I noticed another set of two vehicles now headed my way. I stopped running and stood with one leg slightly in the travel lane of the highway and began waving my arms and hands and even waving my blanket to try to get their attention. I was screaming "help, please call the police" as I waived and jumped for their attention. Once again I was surprised. Both cars had moved over into their passing lane to avoid me. They never slowed down or took notice of me other than to move over to avoid me. I guessed that I didn't blame them because it was, after all, dark and I was an oddball stranger acting weird on the side of the road.

I decided to make a further run for it and cross the highway into the center median. This center median was about fifty yards wide in between the different directions of the highway. The median was covered in both new and old growth pine trees and shrubs. You know, even me seeking shelter among the trees in the center median was a calculation on my part. I figured it would be the last place he might look for me. *Most people would not sleep in a center median,* I was thinking. I ran and ran with my blanket waiving and bouncing in the wind as I jumped over logs and weaved my way through the shrubs. I could feel my lungs begin to hurt! I had forgotten that I was at a very high elevation! I had 15 percent less oxygen to work with and I was about to pass out from not regaining my breath. My lungs felt like they were about to tear out of my chest! It was extremely painful for me. I had to slow down a little and look for a decent place to lay down under my blanket. I noticed to my left, there were some mature pine trees with a patch of saplings next to them. I ran to them and jumped in between them. I threw the blanket over me and panicked!

I was so out of breath that I still felt like I was going to pass out. I was breathing so hard that you could have heard me a quarter of a mile away. I kept breathing like a racehorse and I felt like I couldn't manage to stop! You know, that was the first time in my life that I felt like I was going to die from breathing. I felt sure that if the asshole was chasing me, he would be able to pinpoint where I was just by listening to my dramatic breathing noise. I said out loud to myself during these gasps for oxygen, "shut up dumb ass!" "Shut the hell up, please stop!" I wanted so much to be quiet at that point! I had gotten away, and I didn't have the energy now for a fight. I had no ability to run anymore as it had now been a couple of minutes and I still hadn't recovered from my lack of oxygen.

I couldn't believe how long it took me to catch my breath and until I did, I wasn't able to hear anything around me because of the noise! I had no idea what was going on with the asshole! I really needed to be quiet now and listen closely to my surroundings, big time! I figured he would try to hunt me down and finish me off because, like he said, I knew too much information for him to just let me slip through his fingers. I felt certain that he wasn't far behind me at that point!

As the pain began to subside, and I was slowly regaining my breath, I took note that I was lying in a very comfortable spot. I had gotten lucky and had picked a spot that was covered in a very thick layer of pine needles. The bed of pine needles made the ground feel like a mattress and was amazingly soft! I was being overcome with the strong smell of pine as I lay under my blanket breathing deeply. This comforted me too. "Thank God" I mutter out loud as I enjoy the resting spot and realize what I had just made it through. I was super glad to be breathing normally again. My mind was still racing, and I kept reminding myself to just calm down! *Just chill and listen*, were my thoughts, over and over. For some reason, I began hearing, in my head, part of a song by John Denver. The song was "Annie's Song", and I was hearing the part that goes: "You fill up my senses, like a night in the forest…." "Like the mountains in springtime….Like a walk in the rain…"/ *Oh shit, I hope it doesn't rain*! I thought as the background theme song was interrupted in my mind!

My panicked breathing noises had subsided enough to listen closely to my surroundings. I just knew I was going to hear him somewhere in the distance, but I never did. All I ever heard was the sound of cars whizzing by me on both sides of me. It was, after all, in the middle of the night and there wasn't a whole lot of traffic in either direction. I remember thinking to myself, *if I can just make it till morning, I would be able to signal for help and actually get it. That's what I need to do, get someone to call the police and then things will begin to get better for me. Besides, this guy needs to be caught before he does this to someone else or worse yet, he kills the next victim!* I felt that the cops would be my only solution and I couldn't do anything more until daylight.

That is the point where I felt as if my senses were not overloaded anymore. A tiny moment of serenity had come over me at that point. Peace and calmness were badly needed right then, and I was so thankful for their arrival! I was now in a comfortable spot, in a soft bed of pine needles. I had survived and was unsure if I should be excited yet. I figured I would get more excited when I saw daylight fill the sky in a few hours. I couldn't hear anything or anybody anywhere around me as I listened closely to my surroundings. One thing I knew for sure was, this guy could kiss my ass! I had made the final move and succeeded thus far! As the feeling came back to all parts of my body, I was overcome with a sense of security. I'm not sure if it was because of my blanket, or the quietness, or the seclusion and cover, but I didn't feel nearly as scared now and prayed for morning to come quickly. I was glad to be alive, but I was also exhausted. I knew it wouldn't be long and I would be asleep. Oh, how terribly I needed to get some sleep! As a matter of fact, I had to get some rest and recharge myself a little because the next day was going to be action packed and intense for me as well, I just didn't know it yet. The next day will soon play out to be a day to remember. Hell, the current day had already turned out to be a day to remember too! I just didn't think I would ever want to remember it! Yet, seven years later, here it is in writing, wow!

After all of these years of living with those memories and thoughts in the background of my head, I've learned to live with all the realities of that incident. I have learned to live with all the changes it forced onto me. One of the things I can take out of this chain of events is that you must take account of, and appreciate, the small things in life! Some of the best moments are not the large moments, in and of themselves. The best moments are the smallest of moments. They are the most precious moments that can easily be missed when you are hurrying along in life. At that very moment for me, I was being given a gift. I was alive! If things went as I was planning, I would be able to see my kids, my wife, and continue with a future. I wasn't sure what the future held for me but, I had a future again at least. At that very moment, God was answering my prayers. I also felt great comfort in knowing that I had escaped the wit of Wile E. Coyote, Super Genius!

I pulled down on the blanket around me and got comfortable. I placed my arm underneath my head and curled up in a ball then I calmly allowed myself to go to sleep. I was only able to sleep for about 30 minutes at any given time, but when I was asleep, I slept very hard! Each time that I woke up during the night, I would spend a couple of moments regathering myself and then recalling my situation. I would first realize that the nightmare was when I was awake, not while I was sleeping. It turns out that night; sleep was way better that the reality I was in while awake! I was no longer afraid of any nightmares from that night forward. Nothing in my dreams has ever or will ever top the terror I have felt that day! The second thing I did in the moments just after waking and remembering my hellacious situation was to take the time to listen very closely to the noises around me. I made sure there weren't any new sounds around me. I hoped each time that I would hear nothing but the sound of wind and the occasional car going by on either side of me. I didn't lift my blanket up to look around every single time I woke up, but I did listen very closely to my surrounding noises each time though. A few times throughout the long, dark night, I lifted the blanket up and peeked out for a look at the things around me. I would do it in a very slow and sort of methodical manner. I thought that quick movements could be easily spotted if that evil maniac was nearby looking for me. *You can never be too careful, especially now,* I thought to myself. I am happy to report to you that I never heard anything out of place all night long! One time, when I looked out from underneath my blanket I thought I saw a flashlight looking around the woods just 50 – 75 feet from where I was hidden behind the saplings. Nowadays, I wonder if that wasn't a dream of mine. It's 50/50 on whether it was real or not but either way, I was well hidden and I needed to sleep some more big time. I made myself forget the dangers each time and that would open the door for sleep to overtake me once again. I was totally drained of all my energy and everything I had in me was needing a recharge! I knew that it was extremely important to quit worrying and just rest! This was the very serenity that I was asking God for earlier in the night!

There were a couple of times I looked out and thought I saw daylight in the sky but each time, I was mistaken and went back to sleep. Then, one time, I looked and saw hews of color in the sky to the east. *I MADE IT!,* I thought to myself in a celebratory fashion and began wondering if it was time to get up and try to flag someone down for assistance. I thought about it for a moment or two and then decided to get another round of sleep and allow the sun to rise a little more before I exposed myself. I also realized that I couldn't lay there too long after daybreak because I would be much easier to spot. The cover of darkness would be gone. So, I pulled the blanket back down tight and got comfortable again. I allowed myself to go back to sleep one more time. I was relieved as I drifted back off to sleep. I was so glad that morning was just moments away and I could finally get the help that I was so badly needing. A brand-new chapter was about to unfold for me way sooner than I would be ready for it!

AND, ONCE AGAIN!

If it were possible to travel back in time and I landed at the same point in time as this story is now, I believe I would tell myself a few more things.

First, Go on, take the money, and run!

Second, Have the cops call your wife when questioned.

Third, Don't go into too much detail with the first cops, wait until the head honcho arrives and then go into detail.

CHAPTER FIVE
I Will Not Bow

"...I will not fall; I will not fade;...and I'll survive - paranoid..."
"I Will Not Bow" **by Breaking Benjamin, 2009**

So, there it was, early in the morning. Sunlight was just barely rising over the distant mountain tops and shining through the trees. My friend the sun had come to assist me in waking up and feeling safe enough to try and flag down someone down for assistance. By now my adversary from the previous night was long gone. I'm sure that he thought I had gotten away and found help by now and reported him and his many felonies to the authorities. He, by now, was probably on the run harder than he was before. Especially since I had gotten away from him unharmed. I bet he too was a bit scared at this point. I hope so anyways. I wasn't in the position to make any assumptions at that time though. As far as I was concerned, he was out there in the trees somewhere waiting for me to appear. He could have been waiting for me and looking to kill me to eliminate me as the witness. I wasn't about to take any unnecessary risks!

As I laid there, lightly sleeping in the dawn's early light, I heard a loud engine noise in my dreams. The idling engine began to pull me out of my sleep into awakening alertness. I gathered my wits and started to realize that I was hearing a semi-truck nearby. Suddenly, I heard the piercing sound of air releasing from the brakes as the driver sat the parking brakes on his rig. I recognized what I was hearing, and I figured, somehow, this truck must be close to me. I thought I should raise up and look out from underneath my safety blanket. I sat straight up and didn't yet see the truck but heard it loudly in the distance. I originally wondered if this driver had seen me in the median and pulled over to check. When I didn't see the semi-truck myself at that point, I realized there was no way I had been seen by it either. Where I had been laying and sleeping, it wasn't possible to be seen from either side of the highway. I was well hidden between trees in the extra wide median.

I stood up to get a better vantage point. As I looked all around me, I took the time to slowly scan and look for signs of another person that might be walking or sitting near me. This scan reassured me that I was all alone except for the now visible semi-truck parked just south of me. It was beside the on ramp to east bound I-40/US-66, just directly across from me about 75 yards. I knew that this was a great opportunity to reach out for help. I wasn't prepared to knock on the driver's door, but I figured if I stood by, in front of the truck, the driver would notice me and offer some sort of assistance. I don't know why, but I wasn't wanting to knock on anybody's door just yet. I was still in shock that I had narrowly escaped with my life just a few hours earlier. I guess the thought of startling another driver was scary to me as I had just experienced the same thing with terrible results. I was unsure exactly what I should be doing at that point. I only knew that getting the police on scene was my only option for safety and help. The evil guy needed to be found ASAP and caught before he had a chance to do this to someone else!

I threw my blanket over my shoulder and crossed the highway headed towards this parked truck. As I got near it, I looked closely to see if the driver was in the front seat. I didn't see a driver, so I thought once again about knocking on the door. As far as I was concerned, I was in the middle of nowhere and knew the driver wouldn't be expecting someone to knock on his door. I didn't want to get shot or anything! Figuring the driver was on a quick break, I went to the front of the truck in plain view of the driver's position. I hoped the driver would see me before coming to the front seat and sitting down to drive. Either way, I just wanted to be noticed without my knocking on the damn door! I must have stood there 10 -15 minutes. I jumped up and down, waving my hands and yelled for help at times but I was just wasting my energy doing this. I wasn't being seen by the driver and my patience was being stretched as I watched dozens of cars go by us on the highway. I felt as if I was letting myself down and wasting time with this truck. I was beginning to think that somebody else would have pulled over by now if I had just gone to the side of the highway in the first place. Another couple of minutes went by then I decided to try the other approach. As I made my way back to the shoulder of the highway, I stopped alongside of the driver's door and window on the semi-truck just to look inside if possible. I yelled out for help but knew that the loud roar of the engine would keep me from being heard inside the sleeper of the truck. I went on down to the shoulder of the highway and I made sure that where I was standing to flag for help was in view of the semi-truck side window. I felt some comfort in knowing that I could run and knock on the door if I found myself in peril while seeking help. I also felt that if the driver returned to the steering wheel to resume driving, I would easily be seen and assisted. In the meantime, I had to try to flag someone down along the highway. I can honestly say, It would have been nice if the driver had seen me, called the cops for me, then been kind enough to have given me a microwave burrito and a Dr. Pepper while I waited for the police to show up. Yes, I know, that's a bit of a stretch, but it still would have been nice!

I began standing on the side of the highway, ready to flag the passing cars for some help. There wasn't a huge amount of traffic but there was a building flow of traffic by now. I spent 15 or 20 minutes waving my arms and sometimes waving my blanket at every car and truck that went by me. I did this repeatedly until I grew frustrated. To my surprise, nobody acknowledged me, slowed down, or acted like they even noticed me on the side of the road. I wasn't expecting this at all! I wondered if I needed to have blood on me to get their attention. Would I have to lay on the side of the road in a contorted position, acting like I was injured or dead to get someone to pull over? I again didn't know what to do. I could not believe that not a single person was offering a hand or showing any concern for me as I begged the passing cars and trucks to help me. In the middle of my frenzy to flag someone down on the highway, I hear the semi-truck that was parked take off and merge back onto the highway. I suddenly felt alone and in fear again. As I pondered about how I missed the opportunity to knock on the truck's door, I refocused my attention to the cars on the highway again. I felt desperate again. I felt horrified again. I wasn't realizing that I was only two miles from civilization. The very next exit off the highway was where the gas stations and people were at. I wasn't thinking about my geographical location anymore. I was in the middle of nowhere as far as my mind was concerned.

I was scared and starving to death at this point. I was now remembering the totality of my situation. I was recalling the swift escape from earlier the previous night. I was adding up the things I was now without. I had no I.D. now. My truck and trailer were now gone. My phone was gone. My motorcycle and tools were gone . All my clothes were gone. My important papers and contacts were gone now too. My wallet, money, and cards were gone. All my keys were gone. I had never felt like that before! I was like a lost ball in high weeds! All I could do was hope that the police would take my information and believe my story. It was a shock to go from having everything needed to start living in another city, to having nothing at all. Not even the ability to prove who I was! For some reason it felt like there was more trouble on the horizon, but I continued to try to get someone to pull over and at least call the police for me. I wasn't playing games, I reminded myself, I needed help badly!

As I was trying to get help from the passing vehicles on the highway, I noticed a commercial looking, white van on the bridge in front of me. This bridge was in-fact, the on-ramp for the highway and led right to the spot next to me where the semi-truck had just been parked. I felt as if maybe this would give me a better chance to get help. I thought maybe I could stand partially inside the traveling lane so the van would have to slow down and move over to avoid hitting me. I was hoping that by blocking the lane, the van would have to stop, then possibly inquire into what I was needing. So, I began to run back up the embankment towards the on-ramp again. I turned and ran up onto the driving lane of the on-ramp where I could see the van coming towards me in the distance. I raised up my arms and hands and began waving them to signal that I needed some help. I wasn't sure if the van driver had seen me yet because thus far, the van hadn't slowed down yet! I continued to wave and yell for help in the direction of the on-coming van when I noticed that a work truck on the highway was slowing down significantly and pulling off the highway and now coming in my direction. I pulled my attention away from the van in the distance to the big white Chevy crew cab truck that was now coming my way. The truck had a white, steel, commercial toolbox system instead of a normal pickup bed on the back of it. The white truck was now on the asphalt wedge and driving directly towards me. I was surprised by this as I had just spent twenty minutes trying to flag someone on the highway and nobody helped me or even noticed me! So now that I was fifty feet away from the highway, somebody decides to notice me and help me out? I notice the window on the front, passenger door was rolling down as the truck pulled directly in front of me. I heard the man sitting in the passenger seat yell at me, "Are you alright?", as the truck quickly came to a stop. As I focused on that person and the question that he had just shouted to me, he suddenly disappeared, to my right, in a loud, explosive, BANG! My body flinched all over as the van collided with the rear end of the truck. Damn the luck! The only good Samaritans for me so far were now being punished for trying to help me out! What the hell?

The collision was quite violent and happened just 3 feet in front of me. I had been standing in the travel lane slightly so as the truck pulled up in front of me, it was pulling in front of an oncoming armored, money carrying van headed down the on-ramp to east bound lanes. I was so close to the collision that broken parts and pieces flew everywhere including on me! The crash was so loud that my ears began ringing right afterwards. This money van had just smashed into the rear end of a work truck that had 3 men in it, on their way to work. They were only trying to offer me assistance and now were traumatically involved in a traffic collision, all because of me! I remember thinking, *Holy Shit!* I suddenly realized in a flash that I was almost killed just then. If the van had swerved to miss hitting the work truck, it would have swerved right where I was standing. Right after being asked if I was alright by the passenger of the work truck, I would have been struck by the van, flying to my death 30 or 40 feet away. I cringed at the thought of that!

I hope you can grasp just how horrendous and loud this crash was. Two big, heavy vehicles colliding just feet in front me is something that's so difficult to describe! I had my nerves wrenched out once again! I never heard any screeching or skidding tire noises, just a big crash! The work truck had fully come to a complete stop just before the impact. I don't think the armored van driver had any time to react to another vehicle suddenly entering into, and stopping in, the road directly in front of his vehicle. There was no reaction time at all for the van or me! All I knew was, my body and mind was reacting to it afterwards!

As I stood there, shocked, and with tears filling my eyes, I was horrified outwardly while laughing inside at just how ridiculous all this craziness was getting! I really couldn't believe what had just happened! I felt even more like I was on a movie set again! As you and I both know, I wasn't on any movie set at all. I was living in a real-life twilight zone! Everything around me seemed to be going wrong just like my old companion Murphy would have it. Everything was now starting to combine together into be a big symphony of destruction! *Why?* seemed to be my biggest question after this bizarre twist of events.

Time seemed to drag on and on as I was in complete shock! I know that within seconds, people got out of the work truck and appeared uninjured to me. I mainly remember that the man that was sitting in the front passenger seat of the work truck, and that had yelled out to me just before the crash, immediately came over to me and asked me if I were okay. I didn't respond yet because I didn't know the answer to his question for sure. I was uninjured alright, but I was far from okay, if you know what I mean! He assured me that everything was going to be fine. I didn't need to answer him because my face and my expressions gave him plenty of indication that I was definitely not okay. He was able to see clearly what others later refuse to see. He could see that I had troubles going on that were much greater than just a vehicle accident happening in front of me. He asked me if I needed anything and before I could answer, he ran to the wrecked white truck and grabbed his lunch box out of the front seat area. It was a small cooler and inside it was a few cold-water bottles and his lunch. He grabbed a bottle of water and rushed it over to me and said, "Here you go, have some water, I know you must be thirsty!" I thanked him whole heartedly! I took the water and began drinking it and thinking that maybe there was hope. The fact that he had just been in a vehicle crash and was only concerned about me was so refreshing after what I had just went through! Just as refreshing as the cold water! Thank God for good, unselfish people! I needed this very thing to help me "come to my senses."

This gentleman guided me over to a spot where I could sit down. He insisted that I relax and drink my water. I hastily began to explain that I was almost killed, and somebody has gotten away with my truck, trailer, and all my belongings. I explained that I didn't have my wallet, I.D., or anything! As I finished my rundown on what I had been stolen from me, I remembered that I needed the police to be called. I then laughed and thought, *Well, I guess the cops will be here now for sure! There was no need to call them now, huh?* He knew that I wasn't kidding or playing. I could see it in his eyes that what I was saying was definitely being taken seriously and was stirring him up a little bit. He could see in my eyes that I was terrified and in shock. He felt the realism in what I was saying and could see the realism in my face, he just couldn't comprehend the magnitude of my situation. To tell you the truth, neither could I yet. I again found myself questioning whether all of it was real or not. Was I still asleep under the trees in the highway median and hadn't awakened yet? I'm supposed to look out from underneath my blanket and see daylight now, right? No such luck this time! This was all real shit!

As the reality sets in that I had just caused an accident with an armored van and another vehicle, I couldn't seem to process it completely. I was ecstatic about having survived the previous night's upheavals. I was glad I have gotten some sleep. I had my blanket. I was warm. Somebody had pulled over to help me when I needed them to, and the cops were most definitely on their way! Who would have ever guessed that someone would finally pull over to help me but do it right in front of another vehicle, and then both vehicles colliding right in front of me? Now I will probably be to blame for the whole thing! If the police didn't believe my story, I didn't know how it would all turn out. Would they think I was trying to rob the money van? Maybe I should have just grabbed a couple of bags of money and ran away.

A few minutes later, the first police cars arrived on scene. It was the Flagstaff police department. There were two vehicles that arrived, and two female officers emerged from the two cars. The two ladies started walking towards me and I began to feel a little bit of reassurance in my thoughts. I knew that the police would help me straighten all this out. Somehow, I was going to make it through this. I could see that ahead was a golden opportunity to start over. Although my mind was barely capable of noticing, those two female police officers from Flagstaff were very attractive ladies. They were a welcome sight for my sore eyes! Their arrival had ushered in some new hope for me! Finally, I began to feel some sort of relief come over me. I was excited to get some assistance and get the police headed after the maniac that tried to bushwhack me. I knew I wasn't the first victim and could assume I wouldn't be the last!

I didn't know how to begin to explain all of the previous events to someone else. I couldn't even believe it all myself! So, if I couldn't believe what had happened, how could I ever convince anyone else of it? That's when I had my first premonition or thoughts of *The truth shall set you free.* I felt right then that telling the absolute truth was what I had to do, even if it was the most difficult thing I would ever do! I knew that the truth was the truth! No matter how outlandish or "far out" it may seem, the truth would be what vindicates me. I felt embarrassed about these things happening to me. I felt horrible that I had inadvertently caused a vehicle accident too!

As the cops began their assessment and investigation, I thought long and hard on how and where to begin my explanation. As I said before, I was still in disbelief myself!

I hoped that the person(s) in the van were okay! I hadn't seen anybody get out of the armored van at all. I must assume that there is some sort of procedure for how they handle a vehicle accident with money onboard. This procedure probably prevents them from unlocking doors or exiting the vehicle until proper security steps are taken. I don't know what the procedures are, but I never saw anybody get out of the van. At least, I don't remember seeing them exiting.

As the time ticked on by, the numbness and tingling in my hands, arms, and feet, had now moved throughout my body and even into my brain. Time stretched so much for me that seconds seemed like minutes and minutes seemed like hours. I found it real hard to notice what was going on around me at this point in time. I do kind of remember the two Flagstaff officers walking around the accident scene and doing their investigation. It wasn't long and they were standing in front of me, asking me questions. They were interested in knowing what had led up to this incidence and what had happened during this incidence. So, I pulled myself together just enough to begin the process of explaining my situation. A false sense of hope was coming over me now. These officers were acting as if they were sympathetic and believed what I was telling them. They seemed genuinely interested in my explanation and details. They were obvious in their effort to comfort me. The questions that were presented to me indicated that they were interested in the facts and concerned about my wellbeing. They told me to remain calm and that everything would be okay. They were doing what I expected all police officers to do in this situation. They weren't rushing to judgement or making any assumptions. I was satisfied that I was on the right path now, but it really was a false sense of hope as I soon will find out!

I don't fully remember the exact details I was giving to them, but I told the truth. Things were rushing through my head so fast that I couldn't possibly spit words out of my mouth fast enough to keep up with my brain! All the details were coming to me in bits and pieces and were becoming confusing for me. I am not sure how it all must have seemed to these officers, but I tried my best to explain my situation. The Flagstaff, AZ officers never gave me any reason to doubt them at any time. I was to-the-point and I thought that what I was saying was taken at face value and having an impact on their investigation. I felt as if they might actually be believing what I had to say. I was worried about the devil man getting away and wanted the attention directed towards him as soon as possible! That was my primary worry now! I was lucky to have escaped with my life! I was afraid that I could still be killed by that guy!

I recall the guys that were inside the now wrecked work truck were standing off to the side of me and the two officers. They were listening to my every word as I explained myself to the Flagstaff police. There was a little break in discussion as the Arizona Highway Patrol arrived on the scene. I can't put my finger on the amount of time that went by, but I remember the state police walking around with the Flagstaff police and having a lengthy discussion.

Next thing I knew, there stood the supervising officer from the Arizona Highway Patrol, directly in front of me, asking me questions. He was asking specific questions that led me to believe that he had been given the information about my situation from the Flagstaff police. I had gone into some detail for the Flagstaff police and wasn't sure what, if any, had been passed on to this guy. I hoped that I wouldn't have to start over again explaining everything had happened. Nowadays, after knowing what happens next, I would have been better off telling the whole thing, front to back, to the new investigative officer. But I felt by the line of questioning that he was aware of most of what I had said already. I just stood there and answered his questions the best I could. The problem was, he would only listen for about thirty seconds or so and then interrupt me, over and over again. Each time with a little bit more attitude and authority! It became obvious to me that he didn't like or believe what I was saying. When he looked at me, he was looking over his glasses and his angry, harsh looks communicated to me that I must respect his authority! It only took about a minute or two for him to make me feel like a criminal and not a victim. I was trying and pleading with him to let me finish what I was saying. Each time I would be interrupted with argument and slapped sideways with more questions. His voice was getting louder and sounding more aggravated as time went on. I couldn't believe what was happening to me! I understood he had reason to doubt me, but he was getting very rude and pushy. I wasn't in the mind set or the mood to be able to calmly take the harassment that I was now getting from the bully!

I tried to look at the name on his uniform but every time I looked, my eyes would get drawn over to the patch on his shirt that said, "Arizona Department of Public Safety." I would laugh inside. I would think to myself that it should have said, *Arizona Department of Public Danger!* I never was able to register and remember his name due to this. I didn't feel safe with this guy at all! I was starting to get very nervous again! I was getting angry at what I was having to go through now. I was pushed into defensive mode when I was needing simple help and understanding. I felt the most important thing was that the man who attempted to kill me was now on the loose in the Flagstaff area and so far, I wasn't being taken seriously at all! I was met by this so-called public servant with resistance and attitude! I was not feeling the same vibes from the state police that I had felt from the Flagstaff police in any way! In fact, it all was starting to set me off inside. I wasn't comfortable with the cops now for sure! They were not taking the time to listen to any of the details that I had to offer them. I had told the patrol officer where they could find the car that was abandoned in New Mexico when I picked up the crazy guy. I told them where he was headed and why. I mentioned that his destination was Bally's Resort on the Las Vegas strip. I could tell that nothing I was saying was sinking in with this guy. Before I was able to finish telling him all the details, he got a call on his radio, and he told me to stay put and he would return shortly. Before he walked away, he told me to be thinking about my story because none of it made any sense. I thought to myself that if he would just let me tell the story without interruption, it would make more sense to him! When he returned moments later, he told me that they would be doing a full investigation and that I would be in copious amounts of trouble if any part of my story was fabricated. He was nearly shouting this to me with definite scorn in his demeanor! He then walked over to another police officer for additional discussion. Of course, I was aggravated by this interaction, but I stood by as he requested.

I thought the police would assist me, begin the search for the would-be killer, and bring me a sense of safety and peace to an already unbearable set of circumstances. Again, I was incorrectly assuming that I was in good hands! After all, I spent the last eight or ten hours looking forward to contacting the authorities as I had no other outlet for assistance.

During a break in questioning from the state police supervisor, the guy who originally got me water and sat me down stepped forward and asked me if I needed a phone? He wanted to know if I needed to get ahold of somebody that could help me. He said he figured I probably needed to get some phone numbers too since my phone had been taken from me the previous night. He was right. I hadn't yet thought of that.

He went and grabbed me a piece of paper and a pen and handed them to me with his personal cell phone to use. I don't remember if I thanked him, but I will now, Thanks Good Samaritan Dude! I then called my wife back in Tulsa, Ok, at the hospital where she was working that morning as a registered nurse. I couldn't remember very many numbers, but I remembered her work number as I had called it often. I knew she would be mad at me for not calling her back the previous night. I gave her a quick rundown on my situation and told her that I needed to get some phone numbers from her. I explained how the guy that wanted to use my phone to call his wife had tried to kill me and that I had escaped and ran for my life. I can't speak for her, but I know that with my crying and the urgency emanating from my voice, she was able to tell right away that I was rattled and upset.

Calling my wife was the first step in the process of making sense of what had just happened. I was still preparing for more verbal explanation to the cops as they had only heard a small portion of my story. Being in shock, I was still not comprehending everything that was transpiring around me very well. She began giving me numbers starting with her dad's cell phone number and then next she gave me my dad's cell phone number. During my phone conversation, as my wife read off my dad's cell phone number, I was interrupted by the same supervisor on the scene with the Arizona Highway Patrol. He insisted that I hang up the phone call and to come with him. He stated to me that my truck had been located and he needed my assistance. Well, now I started to get excited! I figured that this was the very piece of evidence I needed to begin proving my identity and my story! I eagerly told my wife that the police had just located my truck and that I had to go. I told her I would call her back as soon as I could, but it might be a while. I hung up and gave the phone back to the helpful guy who loaned it to me. I never told that guy, or his two other companions a proper "thankyou" for stopping to help me. I never told them how sorry I was that they were involved in such horrible collision while trying to assist me. I can only hope I get an opportunity to tell them all of that in person some day!

I was jumping up and down inside right then as I thought, *Hell Yeah! They found my truck! Yay! But wait a minute, he said nothing about my trailer! What's up with that? I should be vindicated now that my story is backed up with real evidence and items!*

As I began to follow this police officer, he stopped and turned around facing me and said, "Do you have anybody that can verify who you are if I call them?" He told me that he needed to verify that I matched the registered owner's information on file for the vehicle that they had located. I replied to him, "Sure, I have someone you can call." I told him that I didn't have very many numbers because my phone was gone. I let him know that all I had was the two numbers listed on the paper in my hand.

As I began to explain who the individuals were, he grabbed the paper out of my hand and interrupted me loudly saying, "I can figure out who these people are!" And he called the first person listed on my paper. And this is where Murphy's Law rears its ugly face once again! You see, my wife had read off to me her dad's number first. This was my dreaded nemesis father-in-law's number that was listed first. So, of course, this cop calls the worst person possible for assistance with obtaining information about me and my current situation! My father-in-law was full of lies and deception and loved to mess with people, especially me!

During the conversation with my father-in-law, the cop briefly tells him about the situation he was dealing with and asked if he knew anybody matching my name. After a very brief pause, the cop then asks him if he could describe for him what I looked like and give him any information that would be helpful in sorting things out. There was a much longer pause then I heard the cop say, "okay", then the silence continued. I wasn't really worried about what was being said because I was giving my father-in-law too much credit right then. I was thinking I really had nothing to worry about, but I forgot how devious my asshole father-in-law could be. After the continued pause, I heard the cop say back to my father-in-law, "okay, so I can assume by that you won't be coming out here to assist him right now?" He then said, "okay, thanks for your help" and he hung up his phone. He looked over his sunglasses at me with a condescending look and said loudly, "Your father-in-law just told me that you have had a drug problem your entire life! He also said that I shouldn't believe anything that comes from your mouth!" When he had finished shouting this B.S. to me, I was completely caught off guard by it! I was horrified and shocked at what was said! There was no reason for this outright lie! Because of this, how could I expect any cooperation from the cops now? I really got mad at that point and had to hold it back. It was a good thing my father-in-law wasn't present when he said that stuff because I would have gone to jail for assault and battery! My nerves were fried out by now! I felt as if I had a huge mountain to climb because of my bad luck and a bunch of bullshit from my wife's dad! I sure wanted to punch my father-in-law and the cop right then! I was thinking then, and still think to this day, that all of this was absolute bullshit!!

My heart sunk all the way to my feet! Despair and confusion had replaced any relief and hope that I had at that point! You know, the false hope that I mentioned earlier! It was gone now for sure. Gone, just like the guy who nearly killed me. The cop told me that he believed I was indeed who I said I was. He also stated that he wasn't so sure about my crazy story. He wanted to know if I were having problems in my marriage. I wasn't sure about his reason for this line of questioning, but I answered him honestly. I told him that there were some slight issues with my relationship just like any other marriage and that I didn't see any relevance to it. My marriage had nothing to do with what had just happened to me! And the arrogant jerk shouted back at me, "YES IT DOES HAVE RELEVANCE!" He continued, "I will be the judge here on what is relevant!" "For all I know, you may have created this big diversion to make a situation that covers up something or creates sympathy from your wife!" I thought he was out of his damn mind when he said that to me! That was so far from the truth, and I wasn't expecting this in any way. *What a complete idiot*, I immediately thought! *Is this the best that the state of Arizona has to offer?* If I had been thinking clearly, I would have insisted that he call my wife at her work and ask her about me and our marriage and my story. He could have found out that my father-in-law was full of shit! However, I didn't think about this and missed the chance to really set him straight! This guy seemed to be determined to prove that I was the one who was full of shit. This was now getting intensely insane for me. I begin pleading with the guy, but my voice had raised a little in pitch and volume now in reaction to his shouting at me. I said to him, "Of course, you would have to call my father-in-law! Can't you call anyone else to get a second opinion?" He responded right back to me, "I don't need to call anybody else! You just need to tell me the truth about what led up to you being here to begin with! Why were you on the side of the road causing a distraction that led to this vehicle accident? I think you were negligent and probably should be liable for all of this!" Then he shouted a little louder, "Now, what happened?" I responded back in a defensive, panicky, louder voice, "I am telling you the truth and I wish you would just stop trying to make me out to be a liar!" I continued with, "There is a dangerous maniac now on the run and you don't believe a word I am saying!" Then, he arrogantly yelled back at me, "You need to lower your voice when speaking to me! Shouting at me will only get you deeper into trouble! DON'T RAISE YOUR VOICE TO ME!" He then told me that by raising my voice, it indicated to him that I was guilty of something! It showed him that I must be hiding something or lying. I thought again, *what a damn moron!* Raising my panicked voice should have also showed him that I had just been a victim of a severely traumatic crime and that I was freaked out and desperate! It should have also indicated that I was now being subjected to more stress by his badgering and verbal lashing! It seemed like bullying coming from the very person that was supposed to assist me! Let's remember, he was the first person to yell. I felt as if the whole time, I had been ducking underneath verbal punches from him. I only raised my voice in response to my being yelled at! Who the hell did he think he was? I understood if he had a little disbelief, but he was plain ole disrespectful and rude to me! What he had just told me made me feel only two inches tall. And of course, I forced my voice back down to normal tone but my internal feelings of dislike towards this jerk was growing. I was furious inside now! But I lowered my voice just in an effort to get him to listen to what I was saying and start believing me. He was wasting time as far as I was concerned. Wasting time trying to disprove me while the attempted murderer was gaining distance between himself and justice!

About that time, he got another call on his cell phone and he answered it. Now that whole time we had been standing by the side of the highway with cars passing by us. I went from being happy about them finding my truck to feeling like I was a suspect in some sort of crime. He hung up his cell phone and told me that we needed to go to where my pickup truck was located. As he turned toward his car he told me, "let's go!" I then followed him in the direction of his patrol car. As we got near the police car, he stopped at the rear of the car and told me that he needed to search me. He asked me if I had any weapons or drugs or anything that he should know about. I laughed a little and said, "No sir, I already told you that I ran away with absolutely nothing which would include weapons and drugs!" It was clear to me that he didn't find my statement very funny. He turned me around where I was facing the back side of his car. He took both of my hands and placed them on the back of my head. He kicked both of my feet spreading my legs and feet farther apart. He grasped and held both of my hands against my head with one of his hands while searching me with his other hand. Then he switched hands to repeat his searching. He searched every pocket, crack, and every spot on my body. After his search yielded nothing, he told me that I was now clear to get into his car.

Well, none of this surprised me at all. I wasn't completely sure why I was searched, but I felt as if it were because he didn't trust me. I don't know if everybody gets searched when riding in a police car. I figured that I would be searched for sure if I were a person of interest or a suspect in a crime. I was confused and bewildered by everything now. I felt as if all the bullshit with this cop just fit right along with all the other craziness that had previously piled up on me. I really wasn't surprised by anything that happened now!

I hopped in his car after he opened the back door for me. He told me to put on my seatbelt and to remain still and quiet as he closed my door. He then walked around the car and got in the front seat of the driver's side. He called in on his radio to dispatch and told them that we would be enroute to the location of my truck. We merged onto the highway going east bound. We only had to go about a half a mile to where there was a pass-through from one side of the highway to the other side of the highway. You know, the spots where it says, "for official use only." Well, he had already made it clear to me that he was "THE" official, so, of course, he turned at this spot and then turned onto the west bound lanes using his police lights to warn other vehicles of our "official business" turn-around. I just pretended that I was a VIP being escorted by security police. I guess I was just humoring myself to ease the tension.

We only traveled 3 or 4 minutes, and low and behold, there was my lonely pickup truck parked on the side of the highway. I was so glad to see it! We slowed down and got off of the highway. He parked his patrol car in front of my pickup truck about 40 feet in front of my truck. There was another highway patrol car already parked about 25 feet behind my truck. Another officer was standing by the driver's side door of my pickup truck upon our arrival. He turned off the car and got out. I was expecting him to come around the rear of the vehicle to the passenger side, rear door and let me out. I was excited to be a part of seeing what was going on. The only sure problem to me was the fact that my trailer and motorcycle were missing.

I was baffled now and wanted some answers myself, as you would expect. I was thinking to myself how the guy must have taken my motorcycle somehow just like he had told me he was planning on doing. *What an asshole!* I thought to myself! I was once again in the position of not knowing how to feel! To make matters worse, the cop didn't come around the back of the vehicle to let me out. He just walked away towards the other officer and left me sitting in his car which was beginning to get hot from the sun beating down on me through the rear window. So now I spun around in my seat to look through the rear window of the police car to see what was happening. I saw that he was standing with the other highway patrol officer that was already there and having a conversation. I noticed that they had went to my truck and looked around it. Their conversation then seemed to drag on and on. Suddenly, I began feeling like I was a prisoner being held in their car and soon they would come put handcuffs on me and take me to jail. *But what for? What the hell did I do? I have just been trying to tell the truthful story of what happened to me! Damn It! Why won't they listen to me? Why am I still sitting in this hot ass car?* These were my thoughts as I sat there bewildered and curious, watching the two cops talk about me! You know, just sitting there in that car really sucked! I was already a nervous wreck. I was about to find out what the cop had known all along, even when he was questioning whether I owned the pickup truck. I wasn't aware of any problems and just wanted to see if my belongings were still in there. I hoped that my wallet was still in there. I really hoped that by the cops finding my truck, I would start regaining my credibility and my story would be taken seriously. *Surely the search for this guy has started by now!*, I thought to myself.

I started trying to figure out of what the hell was taking him so long. I sat for a while, burning up in the sun with no air conditioner. I noticed radio traffic coming out of the police car's two-way radio. I turned around once again in my seat to see the two cops talking on the external microphones of their portable radios. I didn't pay much attention to what was being said on the radio as I was still in shock and still very nervous. Obviously, I had a huge number of things to be contemplating while I waited. I was thinking of how all of this was so hard for me to be calm and patient. I was thinking that I was stuck in that police car while my story was being swept under the rug for some reason. I truly felt like I was soon to be locked up in jail or something. *Why else would I be just sitting here?* is what I was thinking. I then shouted out loud, "What in god's name is going on here?" as I was stressed out to the max! I just wanted this arrogant, narcissistic, overbearing cop to come back to his car and apologize to me. I wanted him to calm down too and allow me to start from square one with what had happened. He never heard the entire story yet! He had always interrupted me within thirty seconds of anything I tried to say to him! Of course, the story wouldn't fully make sense to anyone if they only heard tiny parts of it and not in any chronological order! Again, I tell you he was, and probably still is, a damn idiot! He kept me sitting there, thirsty, hungry, and worn out, in the hot ass police car while he and the other cop probably discussed the lunch menu at the local diner!

Finally, he turned towards me as I was watching from inside his car. He walked towards me with urgency and his steps were brisk. He walked like the head honcho with his shoulders back and his chin real high! His eyebrows were pointed downward towards his nose, and he had a sarcastic, shitty grin on his face! This worried me a little bit now as you might expect. I couldn't be sure if the sweat that covered my face and body was there due to the hot car, or the nervousness of seeing his "mighty mouse" approach, or both! I raised both of my hands up in the window as he approached. I had raised them up in the gesture of "what's up", while making the same with my facial gestures. I was certainly aggravated at that point. When he got to his car, he swung my door open with a show of force! I heard, "Please step out of the car" in a loud, firm voice. Hearing this, I instantly thought to myself, *This Can't Be Good!* When I got out, he had me come to the rear of his vehicle. He pushed me slightly backwards to place my ass against the back of his car. He demanded that I stay put and that I not move. I was very freaked out by all of this, and I felt like I was in a bad dream again. He began to explain to me now that when my truck was located, a used drug syringe had found on my driver's seat. "Holy Shit!" I said outload back to him. The blank, surprised look on my face should have told any decent investigator that I was not aware of the syringe that was found on my truck seat! I was floored by this information! I suddenly understood why I was being treated with such disrespect. This added to what my father-in-law had previously said to the cop wasn't making a very good situation for me now! I again chocked all this up to being par-for-the-course for me! I felt backed into a corner, big time! The jerk cop told me that things were not stacking up too good for me. He said that I should begin telling him the truth this time. He explained that there was drug paraphernalia in my truck and that criminal charges might be in my future. He said all this to me with a bit of a glow about him. He seemed like he was really proud himself! He was proud of his superior investigative skills and had begun to break into my lies, or so he thought! The problem was, he was still wrong! He seemed more determined now to expose me as a fraud and bolster his credibility and ego! I really wanted to punch him in his nose! To be perfectly honest, I still want to punch him in his damn nose!

There was a part of me that could see a small glimmer of hope in all this. I knew I could prove to him that I wasn't an intravenous drug user because I had no track marks or any kind of scars from that type of thing. That wasn't who I was or what I was about in any way! I am afraid of needles to be honest with you. I eagerly told him that I have never used needles in my life and that he could see for himself if he wanted. I lifted up my arms to show them to him and I thought that would be sufficient. As it turnes out, that wasn't good enough. He had me pull up my shirt, remove my shoes and socks, pull up my pant legs, and he also looked down the top of my pants, all while we were standing on the side of the highway. This was humiliating to me, and I hoped that by the absence of any drug use marks, I would be vindicated or at least be treated with a little bit more respect. I had endured the worst night of my life and now I was having the worst day of my life! *Holy Shit*, I was thinking! *What the hell is next?* I wondered at some point if all of this was being observed by the perpetrator, somewhere off in the distance. I shivered at that thought you know! I guess that I still do shiver at that thought!

    I stood there and was badgered and harassed by this creepy cop for the next fifteen or twenty minutes. He was insistent that my story was a complete fabrication, and he told me that I was approaching "obstruction of justice" charges. I really thought he was out of his mind for sure now! I can assume that I was irritating him by sticking to my story since he was so convinced that I was lying to him. He couldn't get it through his thick skull that I was sticking to my story because it was all true! I tried to plead with him and remind him that there was a violent criminal now on the loose and that they had better get to looking for him before someone wound up dead! All this got me was scorn from the cop and being told to keep quiet unless I was spoken to! Hell, that's what I tell my kids or grandkids when it's time to be quiet. I have never told another adult that kind of thing! This showed just how little he thought of me and how disrespectful he was being to me, the real victim! How could I not get worked up a little bit over this?

    The one thing I could be thankful for was that I was not in handcuffs yet! Maybe not having any drug track marks bought me some freedom. I didn't know for sure, but things still were not going my way. He still didn't show any signs of believing me yet. He still didn't show any respect towards me. He had been talking down to me the whole time and hadn't stopped. He had yelled a few times at me, and yet he wanted me to remain calm! I was wondering if someone under duress always got treated that way by the Arizona Department of Public Safety. I wasn't feeling very safe with this particular trooper, that's for sure! None of this made sense to me. I couldn't believe how this day had gone completely opposite of how it was supposed to go. I still can't believe it really. I wondered how I could have more problems with the cops than I had endured with my would-be killer.

I felt the urge to punch him once again but obviously I didn't do that. You see, I was angry inside now! I was disgusted at the fact that I had been taken to the edge of my own sanity! I was nearly killed, all of my stuff was stolen from me, and left without any hope! I was angry that these cops didn't believe anything I had said to them. I was angry that I had been humiliated and treated like a criminal when I was actually a fallen victim of an unthinkable crime! Was it too much to think that something would go right for me sometime soon? Time kept stretching on and on as it had many times over the previous sixteen hours. I was ridden with anxiety even more now. I was anxious to get it all over with. I wanted to find my I.D. and see what was left behind in my truck. I wanted to see if I still had any money or whether or not my keys had been left behind. I wanted to know where the rest of my stuff was at. My trailer, my motorcycle, my tools, and my confidence were all still missing from this equation!

Eventually he walked back my direction with quickness. He stopped by my truck and told me to come over to him. I noticed that his attitude hadn't improved any yet and I was curious if it ever would. I wondered why it hadn't improved yet. When I arrived at the rear of my truck where he was standing, he pointed closely at my trailer ball. He shouts, "See the dirt on this trailer ball?" He continued, "You better start telling me the truth because there is NO WAY there was ever a trailer on that hitch in the last day or two!" "The dirt proves it!" He had begun hassling me about lying to him about me having a trailer and a motorcycle that was with me during this trip. "Are you serious?" I said to him. I told him that I didn't have any idea what he was talking about because I damn sure had a trailer and a motorcycle with me on this trip, and that it had been pulled with that truck with that very hitch we were looking at! I told him that I didn't like being called a liar. He angrily responded to me by telling me that I was wasting his time and that he wanted the damn truth – now! He said that he was tired of hearing me try to make him believe something he knew was a lie and he said it was making him mad. He stated that my story didn't fit because there was no way to convince him that I had pulled a trailer with this truck recently! I shouted back that I didn't know what the deal was with the dirt on my hitch but that wasn't any kind of proof that I had lied about the trailer! I insisted that I had made the journey with a trailer in tow, because it was the damn truth! This made him even more mad. He screamed at me to lower my voice and he told me that he wouldn't tolerate my outbursts anymore! I lowered my voice once again even though I actually wanted to punch him even more now!

This was getting way too intense now for me. I was surprised because now I had to prove that I had a trailer and personal belongings too! What the hell? This was getting way too ridiculous now! I can look back on him now and clearly see that asshole cop was just another Devil Man that I had now crossed paths with while I was on Route-66. He was evil and selfish with no regard for my dignity or my feelings. He had not considered that if I were telling the truth, many people in the area were in certain danger. He was definitely acting like he represented the Arizona Department of Public Danger as far as I was concerned. I'm not sure what kind of look was on my face but inside my mind, I was cursing him out like a drunken sailor.

It wasn't very long, and he got a call on his radio. He began talking into his radio using police jargon and once again, I wasn't paying attention to what was being said because I was still fuming over what had just transpired. He turned to me and said, "well they just found your trailer." I was immediately thinking, *Hurray, now they will believe me!* But for some reason, he was still acting as if he still didn't believe what I had said. This made me even more nervous. I wondered if his attitude was showing me that he was mad about my story being true all along, or was it because he still didn't believe me? I couldn't be sure.

I pleaded once again with him about their looking for the person who stole all of this stuff from me. He shouted back at me that I had no proof that there was any other person! He said I had no proof that any part of my story had actually taken place. He told me he was tired of listening to me string him along with no proof of anything! Well, for me, this turned the heat inside me up a couple of notches. I was most definitely steaming now!

I told the head cop that there were three bags in the bed of my truck that weren't mine. I said that the guy had thrown them into the bed of my truck when he first got inside my truck way back in New Mexico. I asked him if I could show the bags to him, and he paused for a few seconds. I was considering that maybe this was my chance to get more evidence to back up my story. The other officer who was listening off in the distance from us began to come over to the bed of my truck where we were now standing. I then pointed out to the two officers the three bags that the dude had thrown into the back of my truck. I told them that I had no idea what was inside of the bags and asserted that the bags had nothing to do with me. The reply back to me was, "Well, we will see! But how in the world do you expect us to believe there was anybody riding inside your truck?" They stated to look inside the truck. They said that there was no room for another person with everything that was piled up in the seats, both front and back. They told me that my truck was a pathetic mess just like my entire story. As I looked over at the inside my truck, I noticed that the asshole devil man had gone through all of my stuff! All of my clothes and small possessions were upended and scattered everywhere! Clothes that were folded neatly in bags and stacked neatly were thrown into my front seat and into the front floorboard. Everything else of mine was tossed and scattered about the rest of the truck. It was obvious to me that my truck had been ransacked. This backed up my story, so I thought. These cops actually thought that I had traveled across the country with my stuff piled up like a hoarder's house. This reassured me that this idiot cop was definitely off of his rocker! I told them that it was obvious to me that the perpetrator had gone through all my stuff. They replied back to me, once again with attitude, that they had heard enough about this other guy. They said that both of them agreed there was no way anybody else rode in the truck with me. Once again, they were wrong! To tell you the truth, I was the one who had enough of listening to their bullshit! Especially the head jerk that I had been dealing with that whole time!

About that time the supervisor turned around and pointed at me and then my truck and loudly said to me, "I will have fingerprints taken from all over your truck, both inside and out." "If your prints are the only prints we find on your truck, you will go to jail and you will be facing multiple charges!" "Now get your story straight and tell me the truth – NOW!" "I am tired of your games, and you are just wasting my time!" He said all this with the same condescending, arrogant, rude, and loud attitude as if he still didn't believe anything I had said to him. This was now very unnerving to me because big parts of my story that he had disputed with me had now come to light as being true. What was this guy's problem anyways? How did this incompetent idiot become a supervisor for the Arizona Highway Patrol? I feel sorry for the citizens and taxpayers of Arizona if this guy represented one of their best!

Well, all of this was about to drive me insane right then as you can imagine! I kept finding myself in situations where I didn't know how to feel or what to say. This happens to be one of those times. Do I react and lash out in anger to try to prove myself that way or do I cower in fear and cry like a baby to show him that he scares me? Either way, my story was one hundred percent true, and I had committed no crime! I didn't want to let him think that he too has gotten the best of me, but it was looking like I had no choice but to pretend to kiss his royal ass! I didn't deserve the abusive treatment by this jerk! I didn't deserve any of the disbelief or the badgering! He could have asked me questions in a respectful manner. I should have been treated better because as time went on, nothing within his theory was panning out! So much of my story was now proving to be true. There was no excuse for his behavior and the disregard for the safety of the people in the state of Arizona. I rarely meet people that I find impossible to like, at least a little bit. Somehow this joker quickly found his way into the dislike category for me!

The two officers talked a little bit and then stepped forward to the bed of my pickup truck. They looked through the three bags that I had pointed out as not being mine. In one of them they found some photographs that were stacked together and wrapped with a rubber band. They looked closely through the pictures then turned to me and had me do the same. They asked me if I recognized anybody in them. I immediately thought to myself that they had looked through the photographs to see if I were in any of them. They still didn't believe me; they were just trying to see what my reaction would be I suppose. I looked through the pictures that they had given me, hoping to see Devil Man in one or more of them but I didn't. I told them that I didn't recognize anybody in the pictures as I handed the stack back to the "super cop". When the two cops heard what I had said, they looked at each other and the "super cop" rolled his eyes as I was paying attention closely and I noted his continual disrespect! They threw the pictures back in the bed of my truck and chuckled like a couple of laughing hyenas. As they looked through the three bags, I watched from behind them and I couldn't see anything but some clothing, junk, and what looked like trash inside them. In the last bag it looked to me like they pulled up a clip from a gun. I hoped to god there wasn't a gun inside the bag, that was for damn sure! I didn't know anything about a gun! I only knew about a large, shiny, survival type knife with a hand guard, blood groove, and a serrated edge on the spline of it! I had gotten an up-close look at it three different times as you should remember. I watched closely as they dug through the black backpack and never saw them produce a gun. I was relieved in a small sort of way. I guess I had "dodged a bullet", all pun intended! It did make me wonder if Devil Man had a gun in his possession. Maybe I really did dodge a bullet!

To my happy surprise, the officers put all the bags and the contents of them aside, and then turned around to face me. The supervisor stepped forward and told me that my truck and trailer were going to be towed. He stated that I could retrieve them in twenty-four hours from the tow company's impound yard and that I would have to make some arrangements with the tow company for payment and then the items could be transferred back to me. I was not expecting him to say this. He explained that they might need to have access to the truck for investigative purposes and he told me that he thought I had been on drugs and had been lying to him this whole time. He said that he had no proof, but that he was acting on his gut feelings. He said that he couldn't allow me to drive away if he suspected me of being intoxicated within the last 24 hours. Well, as you might expect, I wanted to pop a knot on his head so big, you could hang a coat from it! What the hell? He was now delaying me additional days, costing me hundreds of extra dollars to resume my trip, and letting a would-be killer run loose! But what could I do about it? After that load of B.S., the only addition information that he gave me was that I had to wait there for the tow truck driver to arrive. He stated that the tow driver would drop me off in Flagstaff, AZ and that I could be on my way after that.

I thought, *Is that it?* I recognized right away what a complete failure this interaction had been with the police. I was confused, slightly happy, and I was so shocked at what had just happened. I was certainly disappointed that my own belief and trust in law enforcement was now almost gone. I was terrified at the thought that Devil Man was out there, in the area, looking for his next opportunity to take what he wanted and possibly kill an innocent person! I felt as if he had been watching me, at that very moment, as I stood on the shoulder of I-40/US-66!

After the "super cop" mumbled to me something about an APB (All Points Bulletin) that might get sent out regarding the description of that individual, he walked over to his car, got inside it and started it up, and then he drove away. Wow, I felt relieved to see him drive off in the distance. I took a deep breath in and let it out as tension followed with it! I stared off in the distance with a glazed look. I couldn't believe what had just happened! This time my escape didn't involve running with my blanket, it involved me standing still and watching my opponent retreat and drive off in a car. As much as I hated being delayed and disrespected, I saw the retreat of "super cop" as a victory for me, finally! Something had just barely gone my way, but it did go my way! I sure hoped that this would continue.

Now you would think that as I was walking back towards my truck that some kind of peacefulness would be coming over me. It looked to me like maybe I would get all my stuff back. I wasn't sure because I hadn't gone through my truck to check it yet and I hadn't seen my trailer and its contents either. Despite all of this, things looked a little bit more promising. I was bewildered and confused and half of me still didn't want to believe that any of this nightmare had actually taken place. I began thinking about how impossible it would have been for me to concoct that whole story! If I had acted out that lie the whole time, I would have deserved an Oscar for my acting abilities! How could I have made that up? I would have to be a crazy genius to pull the details out of thin air! When I thought back about the previous day's events, I couldn't wrap my brain around everything. The word "Wow" just wasn't enough!

As I got back to my truck, I walked up to the driver's side door and turned and looked at the highway patrol car that was behind my truck with two officers sitting in it watching me. Maybe they were making sure I didn't drive off with the truck. I had already told them I didn't have keys for it anymore. They were with Devil Man now I assumed. *Oh well,* I thought to myself. I then opened my door and on my driver's seat was that used syringe that Devil Man had left behind. Once again I was shocked! I would have thought that the police would have taken that for evidence or disposed of it as I clearly told them that it wasn't mine! I felt disgusted at seeing it laying there in my seat and what it represented for me now. I found a t-shirt in the back seat of my truck and used it to pick up the nasty syringe. I carried it over to the passenger side of my truck, broke off the needle with the cap in place, and dumped it on the ground in plain sight of the two watching officers. I wondered if the syringe was left there so the two cops that were there watching me could see how I would react and what I would do after finding it still there in my seat. I wanted to show them that I was appalled by the sight of it being in my truck. I yelled out, "Yuck!" and looked their way. I felt like they were being assholes for just leaving it for me to deal with in the first place. I don't have any training on how to handle biologically hazardous items nor did I have a container for safely disposing of the syringe. I didn't know what else to do and I wasn't going to leave it in my truck!

After a bathroom break behind a tree nearby, I returned to my truck and got in my passenger door which was already opened. I sat down and quietly began to ponder the previous crazy set of events and think about where to go from there. Suddenly, I thought about my wallet. I took my hand and felt under the center part of the seat, on the floor, and there was my wallet! I got really excited and quickly opened it up to survey the damage if any. Unfortunately, the guy had found my wallet and took the cash that was inside of it. Nothing else was gone except the cash. I was glad to find my wallet and now I had my I.D. and credit cards. I genuinely felt like I was "somebody" once again. I was a little angry he had gotten away with my cash, but I figured I was lucky that he hadn't gotten more from me. As I sat there in a daze, I also recalled putting my spare ignition keys in a slot just above my radio, in the dash just above it. I grinned a little and took my hand and felt inside this particular slot and there was my spare truck keys! Yay! I was missing all my other keys, but I now had a key to start the truck now! I would have needed to have a locksmith come out and make a key which would have cost a lot of money. Now that wouldn't be a problem.

Within a few minutes, I also remembered that I had tucked away a twenty-dollar bill in one of the pockets inside my wallet. I quickly checked my wallet and found that my twenty was still there! I pulled it out and straightened it flat and held it up in the sunlight. It wasn't much but it guaranteed me that I could eat something as soon as I found some food. I was thirsty and starving for sure now! I felt better and started hoping for more positive things to be heading my way.

As it turns out, my attention was helped along by a couple of freight trains that went by me on the tracks right next to the highway. I heard the powerful engines churning their way up the mountain into Flagstaff. The magnificent trains were a beautiful sight for me. My senses were now being filled with much better things. I have always enjoyed trains even as a young boy. They are so big, heavy, and powerful. I am in awe when I am next to a train. As the trains rolled past me and blew their horns, I would watch every car that went by. I listened to the clickity-clack, clickity-clack, clickity-clack and watched the railroad ties push down into the supporting gravel as each set of wheels lumbered over them. It was like a mechanical symphony playing lots of rhythms and noises for me. The noise and commotion pulled my thoughts away from my situation and I focused in on the subtleties of the railroad and it's wonderful trains. One of the two trains was long enough that it had additional engines on the tail end of the train, pushing it up the slope from the backside of the train. I heard the normal clickity-clack, clickity-clack when gradually I began hearing a loud roar coming toward me in the distance. As the end of this train finally got to where I was at, the engines on the rear of the train were going full throttle and they were very loud! The whole ground around me was vibrating heavily as the powerful engines slaved past me on the track. How could I not be impressed by this? I didn't know how long it would be before the tow truck driver would show up, but I began thinking positive thoughts again. The trains had been a great distraction for me after my nerves had been destroyed so badly just minutes and hours before. No matter how hard I tried to understand things, the more I kept asking myself,

What The Hell Just Happened?

AND, ONCE AGAIN!

If it were possible to travel back in time and I landed at the same point in time as this story is now, I believe I would tell myself a few things.

First, Don't worry about making sense of everything. Time will bring better days.

Second, Get the name of the "super cop" from the tow truck driver. Also get as much information from tow truck driver as possible, especially about the cop's radio conversations.

Third, Replace the trailer tires before leaving Pahrump, NV.

CHAPTER SIX
Last Resort

"...can't go on, living this way, nothing's alright!"
"Last Resort" **by Papa Roach, 2000**

I am now at the point in my story where I can say to you that my real danger was behind me, but I had no reason to feel safe enough to put my guard down completely. I couldn't relax in any way at that time. As I sat there in my pickup truck waiting for the tow truck to arrive, I noticed that my thoughts were now slowing down and weren't being rushed with panic and helplessness anymore. I was glad to be void of panic, and I certainly hoped that this would continue for me. I still couldn't really process everything that had just happened to me. I wasn't very comfortable with being watched from behind by a couple of highway patrol officers. I wasn't being detained or arrested but it felt like I was. I simply couldn't understand why, after all the things within my story that had been found to be true, I was being treated like a criminal or sub-standard! I soon found myself reflecting on the last days events. I began figuring out that the disbelief, and my mistreatment from the police, had left me just as stunned and horrified as the terrifying attacks from the would-be killer! I wondered if that was normal for people in my situation or not. I felt as if maybe I deserved the mistreatment and just hadn't wrapped my brain around it yet. At the same time, I also felt that maybe all the BS I had just received from the cops was not at all what I would have ever expected from fair, unbiased law enforcement officers. The public servants in Arizona on that day were not there to help me at all! The general public inside of Arizona wasn't being kept safe either with the criminal maniac still free to terrorize or kill someone else! I wanted to scream out loud in frustration as I sat there next to the busy highway, being observed, and watched like I was a dog in a cage.

It wasn't long and I began to think about that crazy creep that was now on the loose. I looked all around me in every direction trying to see if there was anybody watching me off in the distance. I couldn't help but imagine the guy sneaking up on the two cops and killing them just before coming after me. Suddenly I felt a small amount of relief about the cops being behind me with their guns! I had no idea where my attacker was at nor what he was up to. Was he planning on following and tracking me? Was he going to ambush me and finish me off? I had no way to remove the worries of being killed from my thoughts! All I could do is keep track of everything that was going on around me like a paranoid weirdo now! Part of me knew that paranoia would be with me for a while, or at least until I was able to get away from Flagstaff, AZ in a day or two. I sat there caught between anger and mental pain! I wished for the tow truck to arrive very soon. I couldn't envision what was ahead for me, but I knew anything was better than what I had just endured! Anything but just sitting there, that is! I just needed to get away from the highway and start regaining my life back, little by little.

I sat there looking at the chaotic mess left behind in my truck by the crazy idiot. I was disgusted at what had become of all my belongings. I had originally stacked everything neatly and organized in the back seat area of my extended cab pickup truck. Now my truck looked like a hoarders' truck with everything upended and tossed about my entire cab. It took only a few seconds for me to remember how lucky I was to even be sitting there. I suddenly felt like the mess that I had to go through and clean up was not such a big deal at all. I began to try to take account of all the positive things I had going for me right then. It was hard to find much good at that time, but I knew that my life and future were going to stay intact at the least.

I began the process of moving my scattered items from the front seat area to the back seat area. I wasn't worried about making it neat again, I just wanted to make the front of my truck clutter free while I sat there waiting. Another fifteen minutes passed by when suddenly I heard a loud diesel engine right next to me. I looked up to see a tow truck pulling up in front of me. I wasn't sure exactly what to do so I got out of my truck and watched as the driver backed in close to the front of my truck. I once again did a slow scan of my surroundings to see if anybody was watching in the distance somewhere. I felt sure that the deranged maniac was somewhere watching everything that was going on. I just hoped that the devil man would not be able to read the signage on the side of the tow truck. I figured if he could read the information on the door, he would have a location to wait for me, and ambush me! I surely didn't want that to happen, but I wasn't able to ignore the fear of running into my attacker again! None of my visual scanning would prove helpful in comforting me at all.

As my slow scan moved toward the rear of my truck, I saw the two cops approaching from their vehicle. I stayed in place where I was standing as the two highway patrol officers approached the tow truck driver and began a discussion with him. Within two or three minutes, the officers left the tow truck and returned to their patrol car. They started their car's engine and then drove off leaving me standing there looking at the tow truck driver, wondering what was next. I was really confused, really hungry, really thirsty, and couldn't wait to get away from the side of that dreadful highway!

Right then, in that moment, I had no idea what was appropriate or what I was expected to do. Once again, I found myself in an unfamiliar situation. As I looked all around myself, waiting for some sort of que from the tow truck guy, I recognized the tension that was pinned up inside of me. I decided to take three deep breaths and I swallowed really hard to try and clear my dry throat. Within about ten or fifteen seconds, I made the first move and asked the driver if I was supposed to wait nearby or climb into the tow truck to wait. He was quick to respond to me and he told me to just stand way back, out of the way. He stated that he would have to turn his tow truck around and grab my pickup truck from the rear end to tow it. He said that once he had completed hooking up to my truck and he was ready to leave, he would let me know when I was clear to get into his tow truck.

Well, that solved my first question. I definitely knew what was expected from me now. I originally thought that he was showing signs of not trusting me but now that I have had plenty of time to think about it all, I don't think my instructions from him were based on anything personal at all. I didn't think about him maintaining his own safety by not having me inside his truck while he worked outside of it to connect to my pickup truck. I hadn't considered that there were remote controls for all of the exterior towing equipment and apparatus just inside the cab of the tow truck. It was much safer for the driver to keep me back, out of danger, and out of the cab of his truck until he was finished and was safely inside his cab.

I stood way back to the side of the road as I watched him turn on his flashing yellow lights. He then turned his tow truck around when the traffic allowed it, and he slowly backed up the tow truck towards the rear end of my pickup truck. After he had put on the necessary straps and chains to secure my truck, he then wrapped my driver's side seatbelt around the steering wheel to keep my front tires from turning while the vehicle was being towed. As he climbed into the cab of the tow truck, he shouted at me that I was good to get inside of the tow truck with him.

I had a sudden inrush of various thoughts which included the relief and happiness that I was feeling just to be able to finally get away from the side of the damn highway! I had been there way too long at that point, and I was completely terrified of running into my would-be killer out there! I was also considering how nervous I was about getting inside another vehicle right next to a stranger after I just had such bad luck doing the same thing just hours earlier! I was sweating and shaking about those thoughts. The main thing that was running through my head as I prepared to climb into the tow truck was that I really needed to talk to somebody that was non-threatening, and neutral! I was sure hoping he would be neutral to me! I also needed some information to help me process everything that had just happened to me. He would be the first person available to me to converse with and initiate the process of assimilation.

When I got in and secured my seatbelt, I became uncomfortable about having to start over, once again, and establish a rapport with a stranger for the purpose of a conversation. It had been less than twenty-four hours since having to go through the same procedure with devil man and the resulting situation was not very favorable for me! I wasn't stupid! I knew that situation would not likely lead to anything dangerous for me but of course, the thought wouldn't leave the front of my consciousness! The obvious fact was that I didn't know that person at all and I was unsure where our conversations would be headed, so I chose to just remain silent and not say anything at first. I really didn't know how to start out the conversation and was hoping the driver would be the one to break the ice, so to speak.

He quickly started the engine and put the gear shifter into drive. As soon as the traffic cleared enough for him, he pulled out and made a U-turn, and then merged onto the interstate headed west toward the next exit in Flagstaff. Within a minute or two, the silence and my curiosity got the best of me, and I initiated a few questions to the driver after introducing myself and giving him my name. The first thing I asked him was how much did he know about me and my situation. I unexpectedly was greeted with a roll of laughter. At first, I was sort of insulted by the laughter. I didn't find anything funny about what I had just endured! Nothing at all! When he stopped his chuckling, he then told me that I had been talked about quite a bit on the scanner that he keeps with him. He said that he had been listening to and following along with the radio chatter between the various police agencies all morning long. I was a little surprised by this. He then turned his head towards me and looked directly into my eyes as he said to me in a firm voice, "mister, you've been the big news around here this morning!" He also told me that he hadn't heard that much dramatic radio chatter in a long time. He said that it was welcome though because it had been slow and boring around Flagstaff, AZ lately.

I asked the driver again if he knew any of the details surrounding what had happened to me. He told me that he really didn't know much or remember many of the details that was discussed on the police radios. He stated that all he knew for sure was that he was instructed to take my pickup truck and trailer to his tow yard and lock them up until the next day. He told me that on the way back from picking up my trailer, he would be dropping me off just down the street from the tow company's gated entrance. I asked him about where I was supposed to go from there and he told me that he was just releasing me and that is where we both would part. No further explanation was offered but I understood his position.

I explained to him that I really didn't understand what was going on exactly. I told him that the Flagstaff police were helpful and cool, however the state police treated me like I was a criminal and a jerk! I wound up telling him that I had been taken hostage and nearly killed by a stranded motorist that I had tried to help. I explained that the state police didn't believe a word I had said to them and that they had let a deranged, drug addicted killer go loose without any thought to the safety of the people in the area! I told him that my situation with the highway patrol was so horrible and stressful that it had left me just as frazzled as when I had to fight for my life from my attacker. There was a little bit of a pause right after I said that. He then responded to me, "You know, the guy that you are talking about with the Arizona Highway Patrol just happens to be the area training supervisor for the state police." He told me how that guy was an extremely arrogant person and said that he thought highly of himself. "In fact," He said, "He thinks that he's God's gift to all police officers." He restated to me that he didn't know much about my story, but he knew what that guy was like. He told me that I would be a little easier to believe than that loudmouth cop as far as he was concerned! He told me that I was lucky that he didn't try to do more to me or create more hell for me. He said that the cop was very set in his ways and that he was many people's worst nightmare! I definitely believed him whole heartedly and related to what he was saying because that cop was the second of two of the worst nightmares in my life! I guess I felt a little better knowing that his arrogant verbal attacks and horrible attitude wasn't just directed towards me or caused by me personally. I got the feeling that there were many other people who had been treated the same as I had by this particular officer. It seemed plausible that he was just a bad apple in a bunch of good, decent cops! I certainly hoped that the other cops were good and decent!

I felt a little better realizing that the tow truck driver had opened up to me and showed respect towards me. I was glad to see that he was confiding in me and showing his true and private opinions of that cop. I was comforted by the fact that he hadn't treated me like a criminal or an idiot. I know that I didn't have much to go on to feel this way but when you've been through what I had just went through, having decency and respect meant the world to me! This guy used common sense and logic while talking to me without showing too much emotion. This was how I knew he was being honest with me. He helped me begin to feel normal again – Hallelujah!

As we were driving along towards the tow facility, I kept a close eye on the surroundings watching for any signs of the crazy devil man lurking somewhere in the distance. I felt as if he were going to jump out or appear at any moment. It was like I was having mini flashbacks to what had occurred the night before. The fear would hit me in small waves as I recalled the events while looking out the window. Moments later we were arriving at the tow facility's yard. When we pulled up to the gate and he exited the truck to unlock the lock on the gate, I noticed that the "yard" was so small that it would have been more accurate to call it a "flower bed" instead of a yard. I laughed out loud while he was unlocking the gate. I would estimate the yard to be about fifty feet by fifty feet square. It had a chain link fence around it with one row of barbed wire on the top of it. I kept my humorous thoughts to myself though and didn't say anything to him because he was the first person in a while to be nice and decent to me. I didn't want to change that by insulting him.

After backing my pickup truck tightly into the corner of the lot he quickly unhooked it and we pulled away stopping only to relock the gate on the way out. As we headed away from the tow yard I began to wonder where my trailer was located at and if all of my stuff would be still on it. I really hoped that he would ask me if I needed to stop at a convenience store or something. I had my twenty-dollar bill on me, and I was super thirsty and very hungry. I didn't want to be rude or pushy, so I politely sat and watched as the few available stores disappeared behind us as we were going down the road.

We got off the interstate at the very next exit and then he made several turns. I was unfamiliar with the roads near and around Flagstaff and it was a little overcast by this point. All of that made my sense of direction completely messed up as we were winding around curvy roads. Suddenly I saw a highway patrol car sitting on the side of the road just ahead of us. As we approached the patrol car I was able to clearly see that my trailer was in the middle of a field next to the patrol car. The good news was that I could see that all of my possessions and motorcycle were still on my trailer! Hallelujah Again!

As we pulled up along side of the cop car and parked in front of it, I could make out that my truck had been driven through a 5-tier barbed wire fence and then the trailer was dropped in the field. Devil man then drove my pickup truck back through the 5-tier barbed wire fence once again, and in a different spot altogether. I wasn't sure why he wound up at that location and why he drove through a fence to drop my trailer. He was obviously crazy as hell!

As the tow truck driver and I got out of the tow truck we walked up to two more highway patrol officers that were standing there by the busted fence. They looked over at both of us as we approached them and I made the comment, "how in the world did my trailer wind up here?" I was immediately met with scorn and a loud voice. The police officer pointed at me while looking over his cop glasses and shouted, "YOU NEED TO KEEP YOUR MOUTH SHUT! I DON'T NEED TO HEAR ANYTHING OUT OF YOUR MOUTH!" You know, I had never seen that particular officer before right then and I thought that what he had said to me was extremely rude and uncalled for! I wanted to tell him back, "I don't want to hear anything out of your mouth, asshole!" but I couldn't, and I didn't say what I wanted to say. I just showed him that I was mad by the look in my face as I stared him down while I passed him walking toward my trailer in the field. I was thinking, *how dare he talk to me like that! Are all these state cops assholes? Last time I had checked; My speech was protected under the first amendment of the United States Constitution!*

I looked my trailer over thoroughly and saw that everything was still there and in good order. I had no explanation for why my trailer was in the middle of that field, but I was glad to have found the trailer and even more glad that all of my stuff was still there on it. Thank God, once again!

The tow driver got a tool out of one of his toolboxes and cut the five barbed wires and pulled them over to the side with enough room to allow us to drive through the fence without damaging his truck or mine, or their tires. He pulled around my trailer then backed carefully up to its tongue. He then hitched it to his truck and fastened the trailer light connectors. The next thing I knew, we were driving out of the dirty, dusty field and back onto the pavement. Then within 30 seconds, he made a right turn onto a long road that led to the on ramp to I-40 West. It was only a quarter of a mile down the interstate from this on ramp where my pickup truck had run out of gas earlier, and forced the devil man to abandon it. This proves or shows why my trailer ball had dirt on it huh? I wished the original asshole cop was there for me to point out his stupidity regarding dirt being on my trailer ball!

Within a few minutes, we were approaching the entrance to the tow company's building and impound yard. He asked me if dropping me off at the street corner by the office was okay with me. I really was hoping that he would drop me off at a store of some place to eat but I agreed that dropping me off at that spot was fine. This was because I was trying to show my gratitude by just being cordial and polite. I didn't have any expectations at that point about anything! As he pulled up to the end of the street where he was planning on dropping me off, he handed me a business card for the towing company. He wrote his cell phone number on the back and told me to call the number on the front of the card the next day to make the necessary arrangements for payment to pick up my truck and trailer. He said that if I ran into any problems or had questions, I should call him at the cell phone number that he had written for me on the back of the card. I thanked him again and closed the door to the tow truck. I then watched as he drove off toward the entrance to the tow facility.

As I stood there and watched the tow truck and my trailer disappear behind the building off in the distance, I suddenly felt all alone and terrified again! I wondered what was next for me and remembered having the twenty-dollar bill in my pocket. I had no phone and thus far, I had no real plan yet either. I knew that I needed to get ahold of my dad to see if he could wire me some cash to help me out.

I wasn't sure how I would go about doing this as pay phones barely existed in 2014 and I didn't expect to find one easily. I wondered if I would have to ask someone to borrow their cell phone to be able to call my dad.

I knew that twenty bucks wouldn't get me far, but I had to find some food, a phone, a money wire service, and shelter so I headed up the hill towards what I could see was civilization. I kept a close eye on everything around me and tried to scan the terrain ahead of me as I was nervous about being ambushed and attacked. I was praying the whole time that I walked around the streets of Flagstaff, AZ that I would never have to see the devil man from Route-66 ever again!

I followed the sidewalk up the hill towards the main street named Butler Avenue. As I was walking along, I noticed the presence of tension, anxiety, and fear as I felt sure that I was still in some sort of danger. I was definitely afraid of my every move. I was afraid to sit still and afraid to walk around. I have lived my whole adult life with a vehicle, and I wasn't used to having to walk to get around. During that moment as I made my way to the top of the hill, I felt unusually paranoid and fearful! I couldn't fully comprehend as to why.

When I reached the top of the hill, I could see the familiar golden arches of McDonald's off in the distance. *Awesome,* I thought to myself! I thought about how badly I needed food and liquids. I remembered how good the McDonald's coffee was! I craved water and orange juice too! I knew I could get my teeth on a decent hamburger there as well, so I made my way towards that familiar sign that was just a few blocks away. Oh boy I could hardly wait! I was super glad when I got there but I still had to do my devil man scan around the outside of the store and then inside the store before I could manage to go up to the counter to order my meal.

After my order was prepared and it was handed to me, I made my way over to a seat back in the corner of the dining area next to a window. I decided to sit with my back facing the wall by the bathrooms so I could see everybody around me, and so that nobody could sneak up behind me. From this location I was able to see the street and most of the parking lot and surrounding shopping center. It seemed that I had selected a dining spot with a great vantage point, and I felt semi-secure eating there. As I sat and ate my lunch, I kept track of my surroundings and watched the parking lot closely. It wasn't long and I noticed that across the parking lot was a Dollar General store. I remembered that Dollar General had cell phones and pay-as-you-go phone plans. I also saw a Walmart sign off in the opposite direction and at least a quarter of a mile away. I remembered that Walmart has money services that my dad and I could use to wire me some cash using my I.D. for verification.

    I finished eating and sucked down the last of my orange juice and coffee and left the McDonald's headed for the Dollar General. As I focused in on the front of the DG store, I noticed a faint outline of a pay phone just out front of the store. I giggled to myself because I knew that the chances of finding a working pay phone in 2014 were slim at best. I doubted that it would even work but I was very hopeful that it would. I figured that if it worked when I got to it, that would be a sign to me that things were going to start to go right for me. Oh man did I need that to be the case! As I got closer to the payphone, I could see that there was definitely a handset on it with a silver armor cable connecting it to the payphone itself. This didn't mean that the phone was operable, but it was an encouraging sign. When I finally got to the phone, I lifted the receiver handset and brought it up to my ear. Shazam! There was a dial tone greeting me on the phone! Hallelujah, Again! *It's a miracle,* I proclaimed to myself! Maybe, just maybe, things were going to start to get better for me!

    I quickly made a collect call to my parents house and waited nervously as the phone rang several times on the other end. Suddenly my dad answered and excepted the charges and greeted me to ask how I was doing. I spent the next several minutes trying to briefly explain what had happened to me and ask if he could send me some cash to help me along. I was so glad to be able to talk to him and everything started to look a little bit brighter for me! I don't remember much of what I said to him, but I know I told him I needed a phone, hotel room, and enough cash to get my truck and trailer out of the impound yard. I told him about the Walmart nearby and suggested that he wire the funds using the money services inside his local Walmart. He said that he would take care of that for me and to call him back in a couple of hours to verify that the funds were on the way.

Now I would have to wait by or near the payphone for a couple of hours. As it turned out, this location had a spot close by that was secluded and quiet with a spot for me to sit comfortably and wait. This spot was a location where I could look across the parking lot and down the entire sidewalk to see everyone and everything that was going on around me. I felt good about waiting in that spot! I just sat there and drank a bottle of water and a bottle of Dr. Pepper while I waited for the time to pass. As I sat waiting, I took the opportunity to go inside the DG store and look at the available phones and phone service plans that were offered there. That way I would be prepared and informed without rushing around when I finally got the cash being sent by my dad. I also knew that I would need to find a hotel room for a night or two, so I used the payphone to call a couple of nearby hotels to check price and availability. I made reservations at the second hotel that I called and felt better, knowing my shelter issues were also solved once I got my needed money. I could hardly wait, and the anxiety kept building inside of me. This added to the constant, fearful, paranoia I was now suffering, made for a nervous, tension filled wait for me. I felt as if I were back in my childhood when I no patience of any kind. The big difference to my childhood was that I wasn't fearful in my childhood thanks to my loving and protective family!

When the two hours expired, I called my dad back and he answered and said that my cash was available at Walmart. He instructed me to be safe. He told me to get myself a new phone then get myself to the hotel and call him back sometime after that. I felt so relieved and so elated that I wanted to keep talking to him on the collect call from that payphone, but I knew it was too expensive and I would be wasting my time when I needed to go take care of my business. I told dad that I would definitely call him back as soon as I got my phone so he had my new number and that I would also call back as soon as I got into my room and showered. I told him that I would love to have a long discussion before I went to bed and that I looked forward to talking to him later on. I thanked him several times and hung up the phone. That's when I realized that I was going to have to face my overwhelming fear of running into the devil man again. Walking to Walmart and then to my hotel was a long, creepy, nervous journey filled with my now typical paranoia and fear of everything around me!

As I made my way to the Walmart store, I walked following the sidewalk next to the road. Every corner I would cross and every building I would pass, I would be expecting somebody to jump out from a hidden spot or from behind the building. This would make me run for my life and I hoped to avoid this, big time! All I could think about was that the crazy guy was probably somewhere in the Flagstaff, AZ area and I was sure he had a vendetta against me. No matter what I did, I could not get rid of the thoughts of the guy. I only wished that I could just concentrate on the current tasks at hand and what I had ahead of me. Somehow, all I could think about was my escape the previous night and that my perpetrator was likely nearby and not in jail! I still could not shake my fear of it all happening again.

Right after I got the cash from Walmart money services, I decided to just get my phone and it's service plan at Walmart since I was already there. Once all of that was complete and I left the Walmart store, I made my way to the hotel that I had reserved for myself nearby. I wasn't sure how far the hotel was, but I knew which direction

I had to go to get to it. The hotel was farther down the road than I thought it would be, but I kept moving as fast as I could while fighting off the weird, paranoid need to survey and track all of my surroundings. Once I got checked in and got to my room, I locked the door and took several deep breaths! That was the first time in a long while that I felt like I could relax a little. It was the first time I felt secure and safe in a long time it seemed. I sensed that I didn't need to be so worried about the devil man right then and I really hoped and prayed that things would begin to get back to normal. That night would include a long, hot, refreshing shower and several phone calls to my wife and family. I reflected on everything that I had endured and began to ask the obvious questions. *What was the purpose of me having such horribly bad thing happen to me? Why didn't I make the phone call for the devil man instead of giving him my personal cell phone? Why did I take that guy along with me? Why were all the events so dramatic and script like? How will I ever understand and process what had just happened to me? Will I ever feel normal again?*

What I had went through left me so fearful of being outside a locked room that I decided to order pizza delivery to ensure that I didn't have to leave my room. I was a little hesitant to unlock the door when the pizza arrived, but I knew that the pizza person wouldn't be the devil man, or so I hoped anyways! I opened the door and barely looked at the pizza delivery guy. I was worried more about looking around outside my door at who was nearby and watching me pay for my pizza. I felt so unprotected when I unlocked and opened that door, it kind of freaked me out. I couldn't understand why I was acting that way! How would I ever live life if I always felt freaked out by the outside world? I felt so weird that I began to not recognize my own personality.

Later on, when I was able to allow myself to get comfortable in bed and drift off to sleep, I slept pretty good as long as I stayed asleep. You see, it was turning out to be just like the night before when I had spent the night among the trees underneath my blanket. My nerves wouldn't allow me to sleep any more than forty-five minutes or an hour at any given time. I would wake up and every time, I would think about my potential dangers and listen closely to my surroundings too. I would check the door and scan the room for anything out of the ordinary. It would now seem that I was automatically doing a safety check while I slept in bed. I don't remember ever doing that before! *What the hell is wrong with me,* I would think to myself as I tried to go back to sleep each time. I would remember each time that my nightmare was while I was awake, and that sleep was my only escape.

I remember dreaming that night about the devil man a little. I have a vivid memory of him telling me that he and his knife, named "Bloody Mary," had killed several people. To this day, I still can't decide whether or not that was a real conversation with devil man, or it was just a dream that night. It was scary either way, so I guess it doesn't matter how that thought entered my head.

Within a couple of days, I had retrieved my pickup truck and my trailer full of my belongings and I was back inside the hotel room. I was figuring out that my nerves being shot, and my constant paranoia were too much for me to handle while being on my own. I decided that going forward with moving to Las Vegas was way out of reach for me. I wondered if this was a good thing or a bad thing, but I had no real choice. There was no way I would be able to cope with everything I had to deal with in Las Vegas after that monstrosity had happened to me. I was afraid I would punch my father-in-law if I saw him and would wind up in jail too! I also realized that I was 5 hours from Pahrump, NV where my daughter, her husband, and my 2 grandchildren lived. The town of Pahrump, NV is just an hour west of Las Vegas on the other side of the mountain range. I wasn't going to come all this way to turn around and go back to Oklahoma without going to see my daughter and her family! I knew I would cherish the time with her and my grandkids and felt in my heart that we all needed a good visit! I also knew that I should take advantage of all the good things I could find now that I had a new, fresh perspective on the value of my own life and everyone around me.

The very next morning, I filled the tank on my pickup truck and packed everything away inside of it. I then made my way back to the interstate and merged back onto it going westbound. I was now headed for my daughter Michelle's house, and it felt so good! I was doing something normal again. It was the first thing I really had to look forward to since my horrific encounter and it helped me to focus on the road and keep my mind from thinking about the devil man too much. This seemed to work fairly well but every now and then, flashbacks would creep into my mind about all the terrible things that happened to me inside that very truck that I was driving. I tried really hard not to think about all of it, but it was impossible not to. Everything I touched inside my truck; I knew the devil man had also touched the same spots. How creepy! Sometimes these thoughts would make me angry too! I nearly lost my life in the very seat I was sitting in while driving. I wondered if the devil man was following me as I drove. I had no way to know for sure. I couldn't keep my eyes off of the rear-view mirror and I constantly looked all around the side of the highway for the devil man.

The whole time I drove down the highway towards my daughter's house, I felt like I was in panic mode. I felt like my "fight-or-flight" mode was still activated and I couldn't shut it off. It all was driving me nuts! As I pushed myself to keep traveling down the highway, I remember feeling like I was in a daze and the road noise was extra hypnotic to me. It was putting me into some sort of trance. There was a very bizarre atmosphere about my traveling down the highway now and I couldn't understand why I felt that way. Once I arrived in the Las Vegas area, my weird trance kept me from recognizing the sights along the highway in the city I had just previously lived in just a couple of years earlier. I knew there was definitely something wrong inside my head at that point. Nothing made sense to me, and I was still fearful of everything around me.

I made my way through Las Vegas and then over the mountain pass on route 160 toward Pahrump, NV. Soon I was at my daughter's house, and I was so elated and excited to see my daughter Michelle and my grandkids! I felt lucky to have been given the chance to live and to see her and all my loved ones once again! I took in every moment and cherished it as if it were my last time to see them. My daughter and I talked for a few hours, and we caught up on everything she and her family had going on at the time. I watched the grandkids as they played and I felt the importance of my influence on their lives. The little ones were telling me the most right then without even saying a word! There fantastic personalities helped me see the beauty in life when I couldn't even see past my own fear right then. Seeing them brought to me new hope and joy I hadn't felt for a while. Inside my heart, I was filled with smiles! That moment in my life was more valuable than gold! I needed the love right then I suppose. I needed to show my love for them too. All of this was the highest priority for me right then.

When we finished talking I decided to get a hotel room in Pahrump because it was getting late and the next morning I would begin the long journey back to Tulsa, OK. I gave my daughter and the kids a big hug and told them goodbye then made my way over to the hotel to check into getting me a room for the night. I was lucky that they had a vacancy, but the room wasn't cheap that night. I just needed a place to sleep that offered me privacy and security and this place fit that requirement quite well. I scampered quickly into my room and hopped into bed right away. I fell asleep right away and began my nightly cycle of short sleeping periods followed by waking up and checking my surroundings. The bed was very comfortable, and I slept like a king whenever I was able to sleep. I was exhausted and I didn't feel like I got enough sleep during that night.

When I woke up the next morning, it was a beautiful, sunny day. The hotel had free breakfast with the room, and I was unsure what type of breakfast that I would find. So, I made my way down to the office where the breakfast serving room was located and made my way into the room. To my surprise, they had a full course, hot breakfast that included scrambled eggs, sausage, bacon, country gravy, fresh biscuits, fresh waffles, syrup, and of course, fruit and 3 types of cereal. I said to myself, *Hell yeah! Maybe things are turning around for me!* I suddenly knew why the room wasn't cheap. I knew that I was starving to death, and I had a long drive ahead of me. Right at that moment, I made up my mind that I wouldn't let the hotel off cheap with my appetite! I ate like a pig and loved every minute of it! I didn't waste anything I put on my plate. I just ate till I was so full I couldn't hardly walk. Maybe I over did it but I really didn't care right then. I needed a good hot meal and didn't know how long it would be till I could eat like that again. Thank you dad for sending me the cash to allow this! Thank God, once again, for all of the little things!

Now, I knew that I was super glad to be alive but that personal hell that I spoke about earlier in this story was starting to rear its ugly face to me. I wasn't sure how much more difficult things would get or how I would handle all of it, but I figured to make it through all of it, somehow.

As I headed back towards Tulsa, OK from Las Vegas, NV, the journey seemed like a super massive undertaking for me. I couldn't even fathom how I was going to get through the long drive, but I kept driving and driving. I noticed that I couldn't listen to the radio anymore while I drove because it was now getting on my nerves for some unknown reason. That had never happened before either and I was concerned about it. I didn't have the ability to see my way through the long journey ahead of me in my mind. I was too stressed out from the thought of my upheavals and failures. I was questioning, over and over, whether or not my memories were real. Oh, how I wanted to be able to say that it was all just a bad dream. Oh, how I wanted to be able to say I was okay, but I wasn't okay anymore. I was nervous the whole time I was driving, and I had to force myself to not look all around me for bad guys and I forced myself not to stare into the rearview mirror looking for someone who wasn't there. Like is said earlier, it was all driving me crazy! I noticed many times that my hands were hurting because I was gripping the steering wheel so hard. I had to constantly make myself relax my grip and quit being so nervous. I would tell myself to calm down and take deep breaths. I tried to convince myself that things were going to be alright.

I just kept driving and driving and my hypnotic trance was overwhelming. I refueled in Flagstaff again and continued on my journey back through Arizona to the east. My trance was severely interrupted by a loud bang that made my truck and trailer shake. I looked into my driver's side mirror and saw my trailer tire had blown apart and had taken out my trailer fender in the process. I pulled over to assess the damage and the situation. I made my way to the side of the road and again I asked myself, *Why does this crap still keep happening to me? What the hell?* I found my tire was missing the tread and the rest of the tire was still intact somewhat. This meant that I could drive it very slowly in the hazard lane to allow me to get to a tire shop. Fortunately, I was only about twelve miles from Winslow, AZ and there was a Walmart with an automotive service center there. I knew it was late enough that the auto service center was closed but I also knew there were a couple of hotels on the same exit as the Walmart and I should be able to get a room overnight and be at the service center first thing in the morning.

I bent down my fender as best as I could and got back into my truck. I made my way down the highway at about five miles an hour while using my hazard flashers and driving on the shoulder of the highway. It took over an hour to get to the exit where the hotels and

Walmart were, and I was relieved to get off the dreaded highway again. I made a right turn off the exit ramp and headed south to the first available hotel that was closest to the highway. I found a place to park, and I went inside their office and waited by the counter. As I was walking inside, I noticed that it was a little bit dark but thought nothing more about it. The hotel employee came to the counter and told me that they were in the middle of a power outage. He stated that they had no idea what caused the outage or how long the power outage was going to last. They suggested that I try the other hotel a little bit further down the street and on the other side of the road. He didn't know if the power was on or not at this other hotel but said it was worth a try. I agreed with him and thanked him and went back to my truck. I made my way over to the other hotel and went inside to inquire about their power situation and see if they had a room available for me. When I went inside the office, I noticed that their lights were on and figured that was a good sign. When the agent came to the counter, I asked if they had encountered any problems with the power like the other hotel. The agent told me that there was power to half of the hotel and that it was off in the other half. He told me that he didn't know if the power would stay on or not, but he had a room available that was in the area with power. I told him I would take it if it had a good air conditioner. He insisted that the air was cold, so I paid for the room for the night and made my way over to that room. The room was old looking and creepy inside! I had more weird feelings as I entered it and turned on the lights and air conditioner. I figured that I would be asleep soon and none of this would even matter. It seemed like there was a presence of evil in this room, but I had no choice but to hunker down and wait till morning. As I slept, I had the exact same problems staying asleep as the previous few nights. I woke up every thirty minutes or so and each time, I felt like I was being watched. There was nothing around me any of the times I felt this way. I tried to ignore all of this and just sleep but it was a struggle for me all night long. I had left the light on to help me with this process. I felt like something was hovering over the bed and was watching my every move. I didn't like any part of that night in my creepy hotel room. I was just ready to get back on the road and get home where I might be able to relax.

I was so glad when morning did arrive, and the sun shined brightly through the curtains in my room. I hopped up and took a quick shower and headed straight for the Walmart auto center just a few blocks away. I was the first customer in the parking lot that morning at the auto center. I was able to get both of my trailer tires replaced within an hour or so then I was back on the highway again headed east. I was delayed by this tire blowout for about sixteen hours which aggravated me some. It was expensive to replace both tires on the trailer and also to be forced into paying for an additional night of hotel expenses. It made me feel a lot better about traveling down the highway with a couple of new trailer tires though, however my nervousness and anxiety persisted.

I again tried on multiple occasions to listen to music on my radio but each time I found it unnerving, and I had to shut the music off to help me remain calm. This seemed so bizarre for me! I loved music and my life had been shaped by music, so I was shocked to find out that I couldn't listen to it anymore. I just kept driving in silence and thinking about what I was going to do when I finally got home. I thought about what I was going to tell everybody when I got there. I wondered if I would be able to tell them much of anything about what had happened to me. I would panic about having to relive those horrific moments enough to tell people what had happened to me on my travels down route 66. I wondered how I would start over. I wondered what starting over really meant for me at this important juncture in my life. I was worried about rejection from everybody and especially my wife and kids. How could they ever be proud and boastful of their weak, failure of a husband and dad? I was beating myself up pretty good while I continued driving for hours. I wondered if I would have enough self confidence to succeed at starting over. I knew that I would have to put on my best poker face when I got home and be strong for my kids. They had no idea what had happened to me and wouldn't be able to understand any of it for years to come. They didn't know that I looked at myself as a failure and a miserable one at that. Although I was wrong about being a failure, I couldn't let them see me act as if I were one. My poker face was looking to be extremely important for me around my children. I needed to ensure that they never felt scared or in danger and that things in our lives were fine. I just wasn't sure how I could do that or if I would even be able to do that. I was going to try my best though! I'm not an actor. I don't like hiding things from others. I am not one for deception but in this case, I had to make an exception. A smile on the outside when I was frowning on the inside seemed like a very small thing that I could do to make there lives that much easier. I didn't mind this sacrifice at all for them!

During the long trip across multiple states, I made a couple of phone calls to my wife. She had made a reservation for me to stay at another hotel in Amarillo, TX while I was driving. She was so sweet to me, and it helped me cope and made me look forward to seeing her again. When I got to the hotel, it was very nice, and I was not nearly as creeped out by this room as I had the previous room. I slept quite a bit better but as expected, I woke up several times in the night panicking and fearful. Each time I would think about getting home the next day and I would relax enough to fall back asleep. The next morning, I eagerly jumped out of bed, into my truck and I was on my way just before the sun rose in west Texas. I guess I was just ready to get home and get away from that dreadful highway again! I was ready for my last resort of going home and hoping for the best! I mainly wanted so badly to feel normal again. I just wanted to be around the people I cared for and those who cared deeply for me. I needed to feel secure and safe again. I wanted the madness in my head to stop! I just didn't know how to stop the madness!

I cried a few times as I drove along. Sometimes it was because I was terrified about my memories of what happened to me. Other times the tears were flowing due to happiness about being alive and being able to see everyone again. I was a mess. I mainly was scared of what lie ahead for me. I had failed at most of my plans to establish a new life for my family in Las Vegas. I thought I had somehow failed at everything for some reason but that was not true at all. I wondered if I was doomed for failure in the future now. I had no way of knowing all the hard work and effort it would take to overcome what had happened to me and how important facing my fears and memories would be for my success in the future. I just knew I had to try really hard and make the best of things to come.

I kept hearing in the back of my head, *The truth shall set you free!, The truth shall set you free!* I heard this over and over again as I neared my home. As I got within a couple of blocks from my house, my nervousness kicked into overdrive again. My fear of rejection from my loved ones was weighing on my heart. My fear of having to retell the story was heavy on me as well. My fear of admitting that I was a failure was extremely heavy for me too. I had stage fright about seeing my own family!

When I got to the end of the street that led into our housing addition, I would have to make a left turn at the end of the street, then my house would be the third house on the left after the turn. As I made my turn onto my street, I noticed my son Hayden sitting and playing on the driveway. He looked up as I made the turn and immediately he leapt to his feet and started jumping up and down in circles with his fist way up in the air! He was shouting, "Yay, daddy's home, daddy's home, yay!" I realized right at that moment as my heart was filled with joy and love from my son, that my life and family was far from a failure! I realized that my plans had failed but a new opportunity to shine even brighter was upon me. My family needed me to shine again as much as I needed to shine bright again! All that I had just went through was just a harsh learning experience to help me focus in on what was the most important to me. My family! I had a chance to be the best daddy and husband there ever was and I was well on my way. Hayden had given me a boost to my new will to live. Hayden didn't know it, but he had just turned a light on inside of me when I was at my darkest moment. Nothing could have been better for me right at that moment than seeing my child overjoyed about my arrival. He never knew how close he had gotten to almost being fatherless. He had no reason to find out about that any time soon because he was just a tender young child. Hayden was saying so much to me without saying anything, just like my grandchildren had done for me just a couple of days earlier. What a glorious day! Really!

Thank God for the little things! And in my case, the little ones too!

CHAPTER SEVEN
The Reason

*"...all the pain I put you through,
I wish that I could take it all away..."*
"The Reason" **by Hoobastank, 2003**

Now that I have completed the bulk of my story, I need to give you a little bit more information to complete my thoughts and to better show you my transformation into the person I am now today. I need to take this brief moment to express some of the more important lessons and adjustments I had to make within myself to elevate myself above the chaos that occupied my head. I hope this proves helpful both to my story and to those who read it.

I wish that I could tell you that things gradually got better after my return home. The fact is I kept falling into a deeper depression and a deeper state of mental anguish. I had two or three years of real hell as P.T.S.D. ruled my every waking thought. It probably ruled my sleeping thoughts as well. I wouldn't learn that I had PTSD until late in the year of 2016. I then had a physical name for my problems, and I had a reason for why I was experiencing them. Knowing this helped me focus on each and every symptom and find ways to deal with them. I had to be patient and steadfast in my pursuit of happiness. I had to admit to myself the personal shortcomings that stood in the way of my healing and growth.

I won't dwell too much on all the negative aspects of my story, but I need to show you a real quick list of the issues I had to work through. Next I will challenge you with a few questions that I think we all should consider closely. Then finally, I will present my final thoughts and lessons to share with you all and I hope you all enjoy them. My quick rundown of issues is as follows:

- I experienced many years of Post-Traumatic Stress Disorder; I might have some PTSD symptoms for the rest of my life.
- I couldn't enjoy much of anything that I used to enjoy for several years.
- I was unable to listen to music for two years.
- I was unable to watch television for three years.
- I was unable to watch movies for five years.
- I was unable to watch horror movies or true crime television shows for seven years and I still have problems with these.
- I was unable to enjoy Halloween for five years, even with my children.
- I felt detached and unconnected with other people to include my closest family members.
- I felt like everybody, including my wife and kids, were constantly plotting against me, behind my back.
- I was irritable most of the time.
- I appeared less loving to my family.
- I had recurrent nightmares and flashbacks.
- I felt guilty about all my PTSD problems and shortcomings.
- I avoided going places and seeing other people.
- I spent months just sitting and staring out in front of me.
- I couldn't sleep fully through the night for four years.
- Filling out a job application was nearly impossible for me because I couldn't concentrate well enough or long enough to complete the long process. I would get lost in the details

which would stress me out completely. (I was baffled by this one!)
- I struggled significantly to recall parts of the trauma in this story. Many times, I would unleash symptoms during the process of compiling this story. Telling this story was the emotionally hardest thing I have ever undertaken in my life! This story has allowed me to get it all out of my head, in an organized fashion. This has opened the door for me to have much more complete healing!
- Whenever I see a police car behind me or I have to interact with law enforcement, I get extreme anxiety and panic attacks. I fear the cops and will probably avoid them the rest of my life, just because of one asshole Arizona Highway Patrol officer and the unfair tactics he implemented on me.
- I hate riding in a vehicle with strangers now!
- One extremely good thing that came out of the situation I went through. I noticed that the trauma had opened a door in my head to allow my creativity to flow out of me like water. I was never able to be so easily creative until after this traumatic event. This side effect is the only one that I am the happy about.

Well, it's time for us to put on our thinking caps and closely consider a few quick questions. I would like to challenge you to come to your own conclusions.

Please listen to my conclusions with an open mind and compare them with your own thoughts. I find it important to fill everybody in on my perspective as it all relates to my story, my long journey towards healing, and spiritual transformation following this horrible encounter. These questions are all directly related to one underlying question, Why?

Knowing all the crazy events that I have discussed withing this story, which of the following things would best describe the cause(s) of my horrific encounter:

- Was this chain of events caused by bad luck?
- After all, these events were the worst things I have ever experienced and the most traumatic by far!
- Was this chain of events caused by good luck?
- In the end, I have climbed out of the hole it caused me and have risen to even higher conciseness and personal spiritual fulfillment. I also have turned all of my memories into this book and hope to help others in the process.
- Was it all a direct result of simple fate?
- Was all of it preplanned and just something I had to go through regardless of the paths I chose?
- Was it all merely cause and effect that resulted from my choices and decisions along the way?
- Was there indeed some sort of divine or spiritual intervention(s) Good spirits and ancestors were possibly guiding and protecting me from death and keeping me calm.
  Bad spirits and demons were possibly there to torment me, punish me, and pull me off course and into a would of evil behaviors and substance abuse.
  I felt the presence of both good and bad spirits and I could feel the battle going on around me and still feel it to this day!
- OR – Was it all just the result of the nonlinearity of the laws of physics as they applied to my particular journey through space and time? (The way the cookie crumbled for me)

After years of thought and consideration about these questions, I have concluded that my scenario was caused by all these things combined! Everything had to come together to form the perfect storm for me. I only hope that I did a good enough job of capturing in words the ways these things occurred and how they affected me. I have tried my best to show just how powerful and life changing these events were for me. I also hope nobody ever has to go through what I went through during the events and the seven years that followed these senseless acts. There is entertainment value in this story for most people however, I hope readers focus in on the many lessons that are contained within the story and use them to help them avoid, or solve, some of the same problems in their lives. Helping others is the main goal for this story!

There are a couple of very important things that I figured out after beginning the process of compiling this story.

The first thing that I noticed was that the more I got out of my head and then wrote it all down, the better I felt! I felt relieved and empowered by the revelation of my encounter. I felt confidence again. I felt happiness again. My wife and children noted a remarkable difference in me once I started the whole process. Gradually, I came to my senses and could finally see the path towards resolution and stabilizing my mental health again. My family and I were filled with joy and hope as I grew to be an even better person, and we all began to laugh around the house once again. I didn't think that was possible again until the laughter suddenly became a household epidemic.

The second thing I was able to figure out was that the bad things kept following me, even after the devil man was gone out of the picture. It forced me to ask myself why this would happen. I slowly began to see that the original sin was within myself! My horrible choices and behavior just prior to my leaving for Las Vegas played a part in setting me up for this near deadly encounter. I then strongly felt like I was being punished for my stupidity. My foul behavior began just following the murder of my little brother. I allowed myself to sink deep into a state of existence that prevented me from caring about myself, my surroundings, my health, and my life. I was drowning in my own cesspool all the way up until my departure for Las Vegas. My wife probably was glad to be rid of me when I left because of the pain and grief I caused everyone. I was depressed and angry and fell into substance abuse and self-pity as a way of life for a while. I medicated myself with various evil potions.

The most powerful and cheapest of these potions was methamphetamine! I was a willing participant in the rituals, potions, and evil behaviors of meth! Mainly because it was cheap and very powerful. I could use it to escape from my realities and stay gone for days at a time. Later on, I chose to participate in the alchemy and sorcery of meth. I was able to have my potions even cheaper and I found the whole process fascinating. I would enjoy the power, control, and the adoration from other addicts. I had become bewitching to others around me. I was called the wizard for a while. I found the whole idea intoxicating and addictive all in itself.

Eventually I was able to see what I had become. The pacts that I had unknowingly made with demons and evil forces had already been sealed! It was a huge step for me to admit to myself that I was a Devil Man On Route 66! You see, I was taught better than to allow myself to be overcome by evil and drugs! I knew I wasn't supposed to be playing with fire that way. I lost track of my moral compass and dipped to an all-time low before leaving to go to Las Vegas. I had spent most of my life drug free and very successful but the previous two years had turned me into an evil slime bag and I had to find a way out of that world. I now have copious amounts of guilt when I look at the years stolen from my life and stolen from my family's lives! I think of all the lives that have been destroyed by methamphetamine and the ways I might have helped destroy them. I am truly sorry!

So, what would be the punishment for a Devil Man On Route 66? Of course, another, even worse Devil Man On Route 66! You know, "an eye for an eye" "a tooth for a tooth", "live by the sword – die by the sword." There are plenty of cliches to describe what I'm talking about. I was definitely being punished and also guided by these horrible events. These evil entities and events manifested and transpired all around me during my journey. I believe now that they were there to rattle me to the bone and then change my life forever! I wasn't very comfortable with having to face these facts, but they were the truth! Now I can see the meaning of "the truth shall set you free!"

I had been given a huge blessing well hidden within a massively cursed incidence of evil and a struggle to save my own life and soul! I would either jump back into my previous cycle of destructive behaviors. Or I would climb out of the lowest point of my life, confess my shortcomings, change my behavior, make things right again, and be a much, much better person in spite of the horror and evil I had unleashed upon myself! I saw how lucky I was, and I chose to change and grow and be the best individual that God had intended for me to be. I love life, and I love people again! I wanted to document all of this for my good and to share with others. I just wanted to help people again and feel normal again.

As I got closer to finishing this book, I still felt like something was missing inside of me. I still felt uneasy and unable to fully relax. I eventually figured out that although I had come into a better level of consciousness, and I had a much better understanding of all these events, I had a hole in my heart and soul that needed to be filled in. You see, the final thing I was missing and had to focus in on was Forgiveness! I saw that I was capable of being successful at many more things in life, but I could never be fully happy until I cleared out all my desires to get even with or harm my previous transgressors. When a person holds unforgiveness in their heart, they are leaving an open doorway for evilness and their own consciousness to torment them and keep their soul off balance. Forgiveness is a requirement for a person to have complete healing and deliverance.

The most important type of forgiveness is self-forgiveness! You must address forgiving yourself and right all of the wrongs you have committed to prepare yourself for everything that follows. You can't see the beauty and value in the things around you until you can see the beauty and value tucked away inside yourself. When I got to this point, I knew I had changed forever! I will never take anything for granted ever again in my life, ever!

I gained so much during the transformation out of this incredibly dark situation. The telling of this story has been a catalyst to allow me the ability to rise above where I had been in life. It turned the horribleness into a blessing for me. A major blessing too!

One thing is for sure, if any part of this story hadn't occurred or happened the way that it did, I would not have nearly as good of a story to pass on to you. The incredible details definitely add to the overall impact that this story has on people. I am really happy about that! I hope everybody finds this book entertaining and educational. When you read what is contained inside this book, you will most likely feel the pain of my story. Hopefully, you can manage to see the lessons and triumphs contained within it.

> We all have an opportunity to learn and grow through this story!
> -and-
> We all can be blessed, in the end, by the Devil Man On Route 66!

Safe Travels My Friends!

Terry G.
2021

"…words are weapons, sharper than knives…"
"Devil Inside" by INXS, 1988

www.ingramcontent.com/pod-product-compliance
Lightning Source LLC
Chambersburg PA
CBHW030359170426
43202CB00010B/1423